Footprint Handbook
Galicia

ANDY SYMINGTON

This is
Galicia

Thrust out into the Atlantic like Spain's storm shield, and dotted with hill villages and dolmens, remote Galicia reverberates with Celtic history. The *gaita*, or bagpipe, is a strong element of Galicia's musical heritage. Another point it shares with other Celtic nations is its rainfall, which is high; in the northwest, it rains 150 days of the year.

The course of Galicia's history was changed forever when the tomb of the apostle St James was allegedly discovered here. Pilgrims flocked to Galicia, progressing from across Europe, as they have begun to do again. The twin towers of the marvellous baroque cathedral in the noble granite city of Santiago de Compostela, which grew up around the tomb, is a fitting welcome for them.

Apart from religion, fishing is Galicia's main business. The ports of Vigo and around provide much of Spain with its fish, and shellfish are intensively farmed in the sheltered *rías* (inlets). Seafood features heavily in the region's cuisine and the 'national' dish, *pulpo* (octopus), is deliciously served both in no-frills *pulperías* and gourmet restaurants.

The variety of Galicia's rural and urban landscapes makes it a fascinating part of the country. The long, tortuous coastline is spectacular in many places. Inland, the verdant agricultural countryside still houses pockets of 'deep Spain' where small farms sustain a traditional lifestyle, comparatively unaffected by modernization and Europeanization.

Andy Symington

Best of
Galicia

❶ Lugo

The most striking feature of this pleasant inland town is the fabulous Roman wall that encircles the old centre. It's an imposing structure indeed, punctuated by 82 towers, and is best appreciated by walking the full length along the top of it. Within the walls thrives a typically Galician tapas scene. Page 13.

❷ Santiago de Compostela

The soaring façade of the cathedral of Galicia's capital towers over pilgrims who have trudged weary weeks to get here. It's a fittingly magnificent edifice, but the whole town is beautifully atmospheric with its granite buildings, medieval layout and lively octopus taverns. A very special place indeed. Page 20.

❸ A Coruña

Blessed with a spectacular natural setting on a peninsula, A Coruña seems to shimmer on a fine day as its typical glassed balconies catch the sun. It's got a bit of everything: an intriguing maritime history, a great town beach, atmosphere in spades and an amazingly vibrant eating scene. Page 50.

❹ Costa da Morte and Cabo Finisterre

The storm-lashed coast southwest of A Coruña harbours gruff and authentic fishing villages that are perfect for exploration a little off the beaten track. This part of Galicia ends at the spectacular cliffs of Cabo Finisterre, thought by the ancients to mark the end of the earth and a popular extension to the Santiago pilgrimage. Pages 61 and 64.

❺ Cambados

This dignified and handsome small town makes one of the best places to stay in the Rías Baixas area. It's also happily the centre of a wine region that produces some of Spain's best whites from the Albariño grape: a perfect match for the quality Galician seafood. Page 74.

❻ Islas Cíes

Forming part of a maritime national park, these unspoiled islands off Vigo were once a haunt of pirates but these days make a fantastic summer getaway with their white-sand beaches and pretty coves. There are no hotels, so it's either a day-trip or you can stay in the campsite. Page 86.

Santo Domingo de Bonaval, Santiago de Compostela

Pilgrim Route
to Santiago

The climb from western León province into Galicia is one of the most gruelling parts of the Camino de Santiago, particularly if the local weather is on form. The first stop, O Cebreiro, is a pretty village that offers a well-deserved welcome; from here, the route to Santiago takes you through rolling green hills and a number of interesting Galician towns. Off the route, to the north, is the enjoyable city of Lugo, surrounded by a seriously impressive wall, originally built by the Romans in typically no-holds-barred fashion.

Towards Lugo

stiff but spectacular ascent into Galicia with a pilgrim-friendly rest-stop

Piedrafita and O Cebreiro

The most spectacular approach into Galicia is via the pass of **Piedrafita**, a wind- and rain-swept mountain location that can be hostile in the extreme. Sir John Moore and his ragtag British forces were pursued up here by the French army, and many died of cold. Not much further on, they found themselves without explosive to blow up a bridge behind them, and were forced to ditch all their gold over the edge so that they could travel faster and avoid being set upon from behind.

From Villafranca, the first 20 km as you follow the Valcarce valley slope only gently uphill, but you are then confronted with a long, wearisome ascent of some 600 m over 7 km into Galicia and the pilgrim's rest stop of O Cebreiro. There will be few days on the Camino when you'll be gladder to put your feet up. In many ways, this tiny village of attractive stone buildings is where the modern Camino de Santiago was reborn. The church and former pilgrim hostel were rebuilt in the 1960s and the energetic parish priest, Elías Valiña, found suitable people to run hostels in other waystations and began to popularize the notion of the pilgrim way once again.

Although **O Cebreiro** can be indescribably bleak as the winds, rains and snows roll in and the power fails, it's atmospheric and friendly and has all the services a weary pilgrim could desire. Here you'll see reconstructed *pallozas*, a circular dwelling of stone walls and straw roofs originating in Celtic pre-Roman Galicia.

The church has a reliquary donated by Fernando and Isabel to accompany the chalice, which is known as the 'Grail of Galicia', after the host and communion wine became real flesh and blood one day as a skeptical priest went through the motions at Mass. In high summer, pilgrims can outnumber locals (of whom there are 31) by 30 or 40 times.

Samos

About 20 km after leaving O Cebreiro, in the village of Triacastela (where some choose to spend the night), pilgrims have a choice of routes, which meet up again further down the track. The more interesting, but slightly longer, goes via the village of Samos (31 km from O Cebreiro, and a great place to spend the night). Significantly wetter than the Greek island where Pythagoras was born, this Samos is wholly dominated by the large monastery of **San Julián** ⓘ *www.abadiadesamos. com, Mon-Sat 1000-1230, 1630-1830; Sun 1245-1330, 1630-1830, €2; admission by interesting tour only, leaving on the ½ hr.* The Benedictines first came here in the sixth century, and a tiny slate chapel by the river dates back to the ninth and 10th; it's shaded by a large cypress tree. The main monastery is a huge structure entered via its elegant western façade. If you think it looks a bit too square, you're right; towers were planned but the coffers ran dry before they could be erected. Ask at the monastery for a guide to visit the little chapel by the river it it's not already open.

Much of the interior of the monastery has been rebuilt: in 1951 a monk took a candle too close to a fermenting barrel in the distillery and burned most of the complex down. Although a Romanesque doorway is still in place where it used to give access to the old church, most of the architecture is baroque, but a far more elegant and restrained baroque than is usual in these parts. There are two cloisters; a pretty fountain depicting water nymphs from Greek mythology is the highlight of the smaller one, its pagan overtones appear not to trouble the monks, whose cells and eating quarters are here. Sixteen Benedictines still live here and run a small farm on the edge of the village.

The larger cloister abuts the raised church and is centred around a statue of Feijóo, the notable and enlightened writer who was a monk here early in his career. He donated much money derived from his writings to enable the dome of the church to be completed. The upper level sleeps guests (males can apply in writing or by phone, T982 546 046, to join the community for a contemplative break) and was decorated in the 1960s with a series of murals to replace those paintings lost in the fire. They're pretty bad – the artist painted cinema posters for a living – but give the monks credit for courage; it would have been all too easy to whack in a series of insipid replicas.

The church itself is large, elegant, and fairly bare. An Asturian cross above the altar is a reference to the kings that generously donated money to the early monastery; statues of them flank the nave. The dome, as with the one in the sacristy, has a touch of the Italian about it.

Sarria

The two separate branches of the Camino converge before Sarria, the major town on this stretch of the Camino, and a starting point for many, as from here to Santiago is the minimum walked distance to achieve the compostela certificate. Sarria is a bit dull; a busy service and transport centre for the region, without a great deal to see. In the old town, on the side of the hill, there's a simple Romanesque church with a charming cloister and above it, a privately owned castle that needs a couple of ravens as a finishing touch to its creeper-swathed tower. The attractive pedestrianized main street that these are on is full of pilgrim hostels and peregrine-friendly eateries; it also houses a tourist information office. Sarria is famous for antiques, and there are many such shops in the town, and also several places peddling convincing replicas. The riverbank makes a relaxing spot to sit outside on a summer terrace.

Portomarín

At first glance you wouldn't know it, but this village is only about 40 years old. The original lies underwater, submerged when the river Miño was dammed. Hearteningly, the villagers were helped to move the historic buildings to the new site, and Portomarín escaped becoming the sad and soulless concrete shambles that many such relocated villages in Spain are. The main street is attractive, with an arcade and whitewashed buildings, and the Romanesque parish church is well worth a look for its rose window and beautifully carved tall portals.

Further along the Camino, it's worth taking a short detour to see the church at **Vilar de Donas**, see page 16.

Melide, Sobrado and Lavacolla

Once the Camino hits the main road, it's a rather characterless final stretch to Santiago, with fairly lifeless towns and villages straggling along the highway. The best of them is **Melide**, the geographical centre of Galicia, which has a very attractive plaza and a moderately interesting church with Romanesque origins.

If you've got transport (there are also buses here from Coruña or Santiago), it's worth heading north to the small town of **Sobrado**, where one of Galicia's largest monasteries has been saved from dereliction by the small community of monks that live there. The **church** ⓘ *guided tour 1000-1300, 1630-1930, €2*, is impressive, with a strange sober façade of squares and geometrical patterning. The interior is softer, with ornate cupolas; there are also three down-at-heel cloisters and the massive kitchen. Sobrado is on the Camino del Norte alternative route to Santiago, and the monks run a pilgrim hostel and also offer comfortable, simple accommodation in their *hospedería*.

The last fraction of the pilgrim trail follows the busy main road due west to Santiago and has little of interest. At **Lavacolla** pilgrims used to bathe in the river so as to be clean when arriving at the apostle's tomb (the name may derive from the Latin for 'wash arse'). Ascending the hill of Monte del Gozo, now cluttered with tasteless *hostales* and roadside brothels, the first pilgrim to spot the cathedral would be dubbed the 'king' of the group. A large metal pilgrim figure marks the beginnings of the long outskirts of Santiago itself. If you're a pilgrim arriving in a very busy period, it may be an idea to overnight just before Santiago, thus arriving first the next morning to grab a cheap bed before everyone else.

Where to stay

Piedrafita and O Cebreiro

There are several options here, all offering similar comforts: cosy rooms in refurbished stone buildings, a convivial pilgrim bar, and warming home-cooked food.

€€ Hotel O Cebreiro
O Cebreiro, T982 367 125,
www.hotelcebreiro.com.
Just down from the church, this offers small but comfortable rooms, a range of traditional Galician cuisine, and outdoor tables in the heart of the village. Book it ahead in summer or you may get bumped to inferior accommodation in the village.

Sarria

€€ Alfonso IX
Rúa do Peregrino 29, T982 530 005,
www.sarriahotelalfonsoix.com.
The town's most luxurious option, this mid-range hotel is modern and pleasant; the rooms have all the facilities (some are equipped for disabled visitors), and it also boasts a gym, sauna and pool as well as a restaurant. Online deals are usually excellent.

Portomarín

€€ Pousada de Portomarín
Av Sarria s/n, T982 545 200,
www.pousadadeportomarin.com.
Not the most attractive of the buildings along the Camino de Santiago, this nevertheless makes a reasonable choice by the river a short stroll from the centre. Rooms are large and comfortable, if curiously furnished, and there's a pool among other facilities. Could do with a refit.

Restaurants

Piedrafita and O Cebreiro

O Cebreiro has several places to eat, all serving inexpensive mountain food to hungry pilgrims.

€ Casa García
Camiño Feira 2, T982 367 021.
In Piedrafita, when the temperatures are low and the wind whistles through the pass, there's nothing like a hearty lunch at this friendly and traditional spot. The *menú* is expensive for Galicia, but worth it, with a wide selection of home-made dishes served by a staunch local couple.

€ Mesón Antón
O Cebreiro, T982 151 336.
As simple and rustic a place as you could wish to find, this is a gloriously no-frills Galician mountain eatery. There's no ceremony and no menu, but it's all delicious, and ridiculously inexpensive.

Sarria

€ Mesón Roberto
Paseo de Malecón, T982 534 024.
On the pretty riverside promenade, this is a solid destination for tasty meats and excellent octopus dishes.

Portomarín

€ O Mesón do Rodríguez
T982 545 054.
This bastion of peregrine comforts on the main street, is a good place for a meal; the food is generously proportioned and compassionately priced.

★The Romans weren't ones for half measures, so when they decided their main Galician town needed a wall, they built one with a capital W. Thanks to restoration, it's still in top condition today; it impressively circles the old town and is the most obvious feature of what is a small and remarkably pleasant inland provincial capital. Attractive architecture within the perimeter adds to the appeal, and there are several good bars and restaurants. The Miño River running far below adds to Lugo's quiet charm: it makes a great overnight stop and is small enough that things like parking and finding your way around seem to work better than in many places.

Lugo was founded in 15 BC as Lucus Augusti, named after Augustus, the emperor of the time. It rapidly became a substantial outpost; the Roman province that contained Galicia had its capital in distant Tarragona (near Barcelona), so the city had an important local administrative role. The main streets in the town still follow the Roman axes. Today, Lugo is a busy little place (population 98,457), a centre for the surrounding farming districts and capital of Galicia's largest province.

Sights
One of Lugo's pleasures, apart from strolling the walls, is exploring the small streets within their sturdy circle. **Rúa Nova** is the centre for tapas bars and restaurants, while the shopping streets are in the eastern end of the old town.

City walls Lugo's walls were erected in the third century AD and built to last. Made of slabs of schist, they are still almost complete and run over 2 km right around the centre of town at a height of some 10 m. Their width is impressive too; you could race chariots along the top, where the walkway is some 4-5 m wide.

The wall has been shored up over the years, and most of the 82 towers that punctuate its length are of medieval construction. If you feel a bit exposed on the top, that's because the upper portions of the towers were removed during the Napoleonic wars because it was thought they wouldn't withstand cannon fire and would topple into the town centre.

Walking around the base of the walls is the best way to appreciate their construction, and walking along the top of them is the best way to see the town. There are six points of access and 10 gates, of which the most authentically Roman is **Porta do Carme** (also called Porta Minha). In some parts the walls can feel over-restored, but they are undeniably magnificent and lend the centre inside their perimeter much character.

The cathedral ⓘ *1000-1330, 1600-1800 (1930 summer).* The 19th-century traveller George Borrow must have been having a bad day when he described Lugo's **cathedral** as "a small, mean building"; although it's not the finest cathedral in Northern Spain, it's a large and interesting place. It was first built over earlier remains in the 12th century, but its big twin-towered baroque façade, somewhat reminiscent of Santiago, is what dominates today. Inside, some Romanesque features remain, such as the distinctive *ajedrezado jaqués* (chessboard) patterning associated with the Camino de Santiago.

The town was granted the right to have the consecrated host permanently on view; an honour seldom granted by the Catholic church, and still a source of some pride; Galicia's coat-of-arms depicts the host and the chalice for this reason. The host is displayed above the altar in an ornate silver and gold monstrance, surrounded by marble cherubs and flanked by angels. Above is a shower of silver around the eye-in-triangle symbol of the all-seeing God. In the apse is the famous and much-venerated statue of La Virgen de los Ojos Grandes (Virgin with

Lugo

N

100 metres
100 yards

Where to stay 🛏	Restaurants 🍴	La Barra 3
Gran Hotel Lugo 5	A Nosa Terra 6	O Figón 5
Méndez Núñez 3	Bodegas de San Vicente 6	O Pote 11
Pazo de Orbán e Sangro 4	Bodegón El Museo 7	
Pensión Alba 6	Campos 1	Bars & clubs 🍸
Pensión San Roque 4	El Castillo 2	Jazz & Beer 9
Puerta de San Pedro 2	España 8	Medievo 10

the Big Eyes), a beautiful and sober Romanesque woodcarving set in a baroque chapel. The **cathedral museum** and treasury is set around the small cloisters.

Praza Major Nearby, the **Praza Maior** is large, attractive, and guarded by fierce stone lions. At its top end is the town hall, an 18th-century building in Galician baroque, a style that owes something to Portuguese architectural traditions.

Museo Provincial ⓘ *www.museolugo.org, Mon-Fri 0900-2100, Sat 1030-1400, 1630-2000, Sun 1100-1400, free*. Included within the museum is the **Iglesia de San Pedro**, with a curious 15th-century door, beautiful Gothic tracery on the windows, and a strange tower. There's an eclectic display, ranging from Roman pottery and coins to sundials, Celtic jewellery, Galician painting and ethnographic displays.

Roman baths Southwest of the centre, Lugo's **Roman baths** were built shortly after the city was founded, taking advantage of the natural hot spring by the river. What's left of them is within the spa hotel complex by the **Miño**. A walkway over the warm waters lets you see the ancient changing rooms, with alcoves in the wall to stash your toga; another room nearby is of uncertain function. The bridge across the river nearby is also of Roman origin.

Around Lugo
The area southwest of Lugo is out of the ordinary; a sort of microcosm of Galician rural life that seems to have changed little over the decades. A web of tiny roads connects a series of hamlets where tractors are still outnumbered by mule carts and villagers still bear loads on their heads. Within this area are two excellent buildings, both well worth visiting. Few tourists explore the peaceful green countryside east of Lugo; the road winds its way through rolling hills to western Asturias.

Santa Eulalia de Bóveda ⓘ *Mon-Fri 0800-1500 year-round, also Jan-Mar Mon-Fri 1600-1800, Sat and Sun 1100-1500, 1600-1800, Apr-Jun Mon-Fri 1600-1900, Sat and Sun 1100-1500, 1600-2000, free*. Set within this tiny settlement is an authentic enigma. Probably constructed in the third or fourth century AD, its main chamber, entered via a horseshoe arch, centres around a rectangular pool. Wonderful Roman frescoes of birds and trees decorate the ceiling; other ornate geometrical wall paintings have been lost through poor preservation. Though later converted to a church, it seems probable that it was a temple of sorts, perhaps a nymphaeum or place of worship of Cybele. Take the Ourense road (N540), turn right (towards Friol on the LU232) 2.5 km after crossing the bridge, left about 1 km further on, then right about 7 km down that road. It's all signposted. The church is closed, but the guardian is in a small reception building just down the road; he'll open the church up for you. Once you've seen the temple, you might want to stretch your legs a little, and a marked circular walk of 5 km from Santa Eulalia lets you do just that, while taking in this unspoiled rural zone. The villages with their low stone buildings and *hórreo* granaries are typically Galician, but the landscape, with its tilled fields, mossy stone walls, and copses, is curiously reminiscent of parts of Britain.

Vilar de Donas ⓘ *1100-1300, 1600-1800; admission by donation (the knowledgeable and kindly warden lives nearby and may come and open it outside these hours if you hang around).* More easily accessible by public transport, the church at Vilar de Donas is only a shortish detour off the Camino de Santiago. It's worth the trouble and is one of Galicia's most interesting buildings. Built in the 12th century, it was modified at the behest of the Knights of Santiago to serve as a place of burial for the prestigious members of that order. The tombs line the walls after you've passed through the excellent Romanesque doorway with zigzag patterning. One of the finest tombs dates from 1378 and is mounted on two lions who are squashing a boar, representing wrath, and a wolf, symbolizing evil. In the apse are some excellent frescoes commissioned by Juan II, king of Castilla and father of Isabel, the Catholic Monarch. Dating from 1434, the paintings depict the Annunciation and Pantocrator as well as shields with the devices of Castilla y León and the order of Santiago. In the transept is a *baldachino*, or baldachin, an ornate carved canopy commonly used over altars in Galicia; this one is made of stone. The church is easily reached by public transport; take any Santiago-bound bus from Lugo and get off at the turn-off on the main road; it's 500 m up a side road from here.

Listings Pilgrim Route to Santiago *map p14*

Tourist information

Main tourist office
Praza do Campo 11, near the cathedral in the heart of the tapas district, T982 251 658, www.patronatodeturismodelugo.es. Daily 1030-1400, 1630-2000.
The office has a small display on the city walls.

Galician regional office
A few steps from the main tourist office, T982 231 361, oficina.turismo.lugo@ xunta.es. Mon-Sat 1000-1400, 1600-1900, summer daily 1000-1400, 1700-2000.
The office has an exhibition on the Camino Primitivo, a branch of the pilgrim route to Santiago that starts near Lugo.

Where to stay

Lugo

€€ Gran Hotel Lugo
Av Ramón Ferreiro 21, T982 224 152, www.gh-hoteles.com.
Lugo's top option, this massive hulk of a hotel is modern with a considerably better interior than exterior. The rooms are blessed with many facilities, including Wi-Fi, internet, and a swimming pool and spa complex.

€€ Hotel Méndez Núñez
C Reina 1, T982 230 711, www. hotelmendeznunez.com.
This grand old hotel is right in the centre of town, surrounded by the pedestrianized shopping streets. It has plenty of period charm and large modernized rooms. It offers pretty good value for this location and atmosphere.

€€ Hotel Puerta de San Pedro
C Neira 29, T982 222 381, www.
exepuertadesanpedro.com.
Around the corner from the bus station, this modern hotel offers good amenities for a fairly low price. Though the walls are on the thin side, service is helpful, and the beds are comfortable. There's Wi-Fi and internet access, and, while there's no off-street parking, it's easy to get metered spaces near the hotel.

€€ Pazo de Orbán e Sangro
Travesía do Miño s/n, T982 240 217,
www.pazodeorban.es.
In a rather neglected part of the old town, tucked inside the walls, it's quite a surprise to find this wonderfully restored old baroque palace that's been caringly converted into a lovely hotel. Rooms vary in size and price – the suites are very luxurious, but all are exceptionally comfortable, and replete with numerous artistic touches. It's by far Lugo's most charismatic place to stay. Recommended.

€ Pensión Alba
Praza Campo Castelo 31, T982 226 056.
This sparkling modern *pensión* is tucked up against (and within) the city walls near the town hall. The rooms are excellent, with firm mattresses and wooden floorboards, and it's run with a gruff motherly air, making it a very good central spot.

€ Pensión San Roque
Plaza Comandante Manso 11,
T982 222 700.
Just outside the city walls, this modern *pensión* makes a commodious base. The rooms are compact but clean and comfy, with bathrooms and parquet floors, and there's free internet and easy metered parking in the streets. Breakfast (in the café opposite) is included.

Lugo
Lugo's excellent eating scene focuses around the 2 intersecting streets; Rúa Nova and Rúa da Cruz. Most of these bars give a small free tapa with each drink.

€€€ Campos
Rúa Nova 4, T982 229 743.
Right in the heart of eat street, this Lugo classic in expanded premises offers a top range of excellent seafood, as well as meat dishes and, in season, game. Prices are higher than they once were, but it's as hospitable and popular as ever.

€€€ La Barra
C San Marcos 27, T982 252 920.
A sleek, stylish seafood restaurant that's popular with a well-heeled traditional Lugo clientele. It's decorated in executive style; dishes such as *rodaballo* (turbot) or *kokotxas* (hake cheeks in sauce) are among the stars of the reliably excellent fish choices.

€€€ Restaurante España
Rúa Teatro 10, T982 242 717,
www.restespana.com.
This modern restaurant serves gourmet Galician food. The menu is short and full of quality, with dishes like beef carpaccio or monkfish medallions on ratatouille well presented and delicious. Out the front is a popular bar for coffee or *pinchos*, with tables stretching as far as the eye can see. Recommended.

€€ A Nosa Terra
Rúa Nova 8, T982 229 235.
A great place to eat, this is a spot to devour tasty *raciones*, salads, and meats in an atmospheric old wine cellar, beautifully spruce in stone and wood. Out the front is a busy and excellent

tapas bar; the *pinchos* are very tasty, there's a quaffable house Rioja, and the walls are decorated with wood carvings of Galician poets and quotations from them. Recommended.

€€ Bodegas do San Vicente
Rúa Nova 6, T982 253 318,
www.bodegasdosanvicente.es.
This low, small and atmospheric deli-bar has bags of character, although the Franco and Fraga wine bottles are a little less entertaining. The boss is always chopping away at something at the front counter, be it hams, cheeses, or chorizos, which are served in the traditional manner on greaseproof paper. At the front are some barrels where people socialize with a glass of wine.

€€ O Figón
Rúa do Campo Castelo 47, T982 227 662.
A little away from the main tapas area, in an attractive location facing the inside of the walls, this modern and handsome place offers a quiet, elegant spot to drop in for a glass of wine and a (delicious) free tapa. They also have a short menu of quality plates, ranging from grilled vegetables to stewed *jarrete*. Free Wi-Fi.

€ Bodegón El Museo
Rúa Nova 21, T982 253 351.
Opposite the museum, this traditional bar is run by a hospitable Galician couple and is gloriously untrendy, with wooden beams and local folk enjoying the cheap wine. Out the back are tables where there are incredibly cheap *raciones* served; the house speciality is *pulpo* (octopus), which is absolutely delicious and only €8.

€ El Castillo
Praza do Campo Castelo 14, T982 255 587.
This attractive café and bar is an appealing spot for a coffee near the walls. It also does cheap and tasty food, ranging from good *bocadillos* to a set lunch for €9.

€ O Pote
Rúa Miño 11, T982 228 857.
Older than it looks but recently done up, this reliable standby pays attention to the important details – the food, drink and customers. They pour a generous glass of wine and you might get a free tapa to munch on while you're waiting for your free tapa to emerge from the kitchen. Now that's service. Great for *raciones* too.

Bars and clubs

Lugo
Lugo's lively and late bar scene is centred in the small streets around the cathedral and around Rúa de Cruz.

Jazz and Beer
Rúa Obispo Basulto 2, T982 250 951.
This intimate and comfortable bar is a Lugo favourite for an after-dinner *copa*. With mellow music, friendly service, and well-mixed drinks, it's a very likeable place.

Medievo
Rúa Catedral 14, T982 242 021.
One of Lugo's most-frequented late-night bars, this is a place of 2 halves. Downstairs, the medieval decoration of armour, shields, and the like belies a friendly bar dishing out popcorn and jelly beans with drinks and coffee. Upstairs is where the music is; it tends to fill up after 0200 at weekends.

Entertainment

Lugo
Cineplex Yelmo, *Praza Viana do Castelo 3, T982 217 986.*

Shopping

Lugo
Books
There are 2 good bookshops on Rúa Bispo Aguirre: **Aguirre** (at No 8, T982 220 336), with a good selection of maps; and **La Voz de la Verdad** (at No 17, T982 231 104, www.lavozdelaverdad.es).

Ceramics
The famed Galician ceramic factory, **Sargadelos**, whose deep blue, ochre, and white creations are very distinctive, was founded near Lugo. There's an outlet at Praza Santo Domingo 4 in the centre of town.

Transport

Lugo
Bus
Lugo's bus station is conveniently located just outside the walls near the Praza Maior; there are services to the other Galician cities and all over Northern Spain.

Within Galicia, regular services include to **A Coruña** (roughly hourly, 1-1½ hrs), 4 to **Ferrol**, 8 to **Ourense** (2 hrs), 10 to **Santiago** (2 hrs 15 mins), 5-6 to **Viveiro** and the north coast, 6 to **Ribadeo**.

There are 8-10 services eastwards to **Ponferrada** (1½ hrs), some going via **Sarria**. **Madrid**, **Barcelona**, and **Oviedo** via the Asturian coast are also served.

Train
The train station isn't too far away from the eastern side of the old town.

There's an overnight train to **Madrid** (9 hrs, €55), and 2 to **Barcelona** (13 hrs, from €77), which go via the rail junction of Monforte, as well as **Sarria**, **León**, and **Burgos**.

Santiago
de Compostela

"The true capital of Spain", Roads to Santiago, Cees Nooteboom

★Archaeologists in the ninth century weren't known for their academic rigour, so when a tomb was discovered here at that time it was rather staggeringly concluded to be that of the apostle Santiago, or Saint James. Christianity was in bullish mode, and the spot grew into the major pilgrimage destination in Europe as people walked thousands of miles to pay their respects, reduce their time in purgatory, or atone for their crimes.

The pilgrimage had an enormous cultural, social, and architectural effect across Northern Spain, and Santiago soon transcended its dubious beginnings to become one of the most magical cities in Spain, its cathedral the undisputed highlight of a superb ensemble of mossy granite buildings and narrow pedestrian lanes.

The late 20th century saw a massive revival of the pilgrimage tradition which has continued to grow. More than 100,000 pilgrims arrive annually and Santiago is today a flourishing, happy place, seat of the Galician parliament and lively with students. Don't come for a suntan, though; HV Morton accurately if unkindly described the city as a "medieval aquarium". Simply walking the streets here is a pleasure (even in the rain), particularly Rúa Vilar and Rúa Nova and the streets around the old university buildings.

Essential Santiago de Compostela

Best places to stay

Hotel Altaïr, page 31
Virxe da Cerca, page 31
Costa Vella, page 31
Hotel Entrecercas, page 31
Suso, page 31

Finding your feet

The interesting bits of town are mostly very close together. The main places you'll need public transport to access are the transport terminals.

Tip...
Head to the **pilgrim office** (see page 30) to get your pilgrim passports examined and pick up the compostela certificate. The process has been streamlined somewhat, but there are still long queues in summer. A pile of gleefully abandoned wooden sticks sits inside the door.

When to go

During summer Santiago is thronged with tourists and pilgrims; if you don't mind that, this can be the best time to be there. It rains slightly less, the old town is buzzing, and there's the fiesta of Santiago on 25 July. If you're prepared to get wet, spring and autumn are good times to visit; there are fewer people, accommodation prices are down, and the university is in session, guaranteeing rampant nightlife.

Tip...
For a good view of the old city, head to the Alameda, southwest of the old quarter, and wander along the Paseo da Ferradura (Paseo de la Herradura).

Time required

Three days to see the city at a deservedly relaxed pace.

Weather Santiago de Compostela

January	February	March	April	May	June
12°C 4°C 182mm	13°C 4°C 122mm	16°C 6°C 152mm	16°C 6°C 136mm	19°C 9°C 121mm	23°C 11°C 52mm

July	August	September	October	November	December
25°C 13°C 39mm	25°C 13°C 64mm	23°C 12°C 102mm	18°C 9°C 215mm	14°C 6°C 204mm	12°C 5°C 232mm

Santiago's past, present and future is wrapped up in its cathedral and its emblematic grey towers. Pilgrims trudge for weeks to reach it, many tourists visit Galicia specifically to see it, and locals go to Mass and confession in it as part of their day-to-day lives.

Catedral de Santiago de Compostela

www.catedraldesantiago.es, cathedral 0730-2100, except during Mass; entry at these times is via the Praza das Praterías only. There's a Mass for pilgrims daily at 1200, and evening Mass at 1930; both last for about 45 mins. Admission is free, apart from the museum (see below).

The exterior While the original Romanesque interior is superbly preserved, what first greets most visitors is the western façade and its twin towers. Granite is the perfect stone to express a more sober face of Spanish baroque; its stern colour renders the style epic rather than whimsical, and it's hard enough to chisel that masons concentrated on broader, nobler lines rather than intricacy. The façade rises high above the square, the moss-stained stone towers (which incorporate the original Romanesque ones) seem to say 'Heaven this way'. The façade was added in the 18th century and is reached by a complex double staircase that predates it.

The plaza that it dominates, named **Obradoiro**, is the main gateway to the cathedral, but it's worth strolling around the building before you enter. Walking clockwise, you pass the façade of the Romanesque **Palacio de Xelmírez**, which adjoins it and forms part of the cathedral museum. Turning the corner, you emerge in the **Praza da Inmaculada**, where the north façade is a slightly underwhelming 18th-century baroque construction that replaced the earlier Romanesque portal, which, from fragments of stone and textual descriptions, was superb. It faces the **Monasterio de San Martín Pinario**, with a huge façade that's wasted next to this magnificent cathedral; this part of it is now a student residence. The plaza used to be known as the *Azabachería*; this is where craftsmen made and sold rosaries made of jet (*azabache*) to the arriving pilgrims.

Continuing around, the **Praza da Quintana** is a curious space, with an upper and lower half; these are known as the halves of the living (the top) and the dead (below); the area used to be a cemetery. A plaque here is dedicated to the Literary Batallion, a corps of student volunteers who fought the French in the Napoleonic wars. The portal on this side is known as the Puerta Santa, or holy door. It is only opened during Holy Years, when the feast day of Santiago (25 July) falls on a Sunday. The façade is 17th century, but contains figures salvaged from the Romanesque stone choir. The 18th-century clocktower soars over the square.

The last square on the circuit is **Praza das Praterías**, with an entrance to the cathedral through an original portal, the oldest that remains, with scenes from the life of Christ.

The interior Come back to the western façade and ascend the complex staircase. Once through the baroque doorway, you're confronted with the original

BACKGROUND
Santiago de Compostela

Relics have been a big deal in Christendom since the early Middle Ages, and especially in Spain. Christ physically ascended into heaven, and the Virgin was bodily assumed there too. With the big two out of the question, the apostles were just about the best physical remains an ambitious church could hope for. But whether you believe that the bones of Saint James are, or were ever, under the altar of the cathedral (see box, page 28) is beside the point; the city has transcended its origins completely, as the number of atheist pilgrims trudging towards it attests.

After the discovery of the tomb in the early ninth century, pilgrims soon began flooding in, and the city had achieved such prosperity by AD 968 that it was sacked by none other than the Vikings, who were never averse to a long voyage for a bit of plunder. Some 29 years later Santiago had another bad day, when Al-Manzur came from the south and sacked it again. Legend says that an old monk was praying by the tomb of Saint James while chaos reigned around. The Moorish warlord himself burst in and was so impressed by the old man's courage that he swore on his honour to safeguard the tomb and the monk from all harm.

Although the city was razed to the ground, Santiago continued to flourish as Saint James became a sort of patron-cum-field marshal of the Reconquista. Pilgrims came from across Europe and the cathedral was constructed to receive them in appropriate style; they used to bed down for the night in its interior. Constant architectural modifications followed from Santiago's swelling coffers, which also paid for the 40-something churches in the small city. This restructuring reached its peak in the 17th and early 18th centuries, from which period most of the granite-built centre that exists today dates. A rapid decline followed as pilgrimage waned and A Coruña thrived at Santiago's expense. The French occupied Santiago during the Napoleonic Wars, and carried off a large amount of plunder.

The late 20th century brought a rapid revival as the age of tourism descended on Spain in force. Santiago is high on many visitors' lists and the comparatively recent surge in popularity of the Camino sees pilgrims of all creeds making the journey in whole or part on foot or bicycle. Although A Coruña remains the provincial capital, Santiago is the seat of the Xunta (semi-autonomous Galician government established in 1982), which has provided a further boost to the town's profile. Santiago today has a population of 95,671.

Romanesque façade, the **Pórtico de la Gloria**. Built 1168-1188 by a man named Master Mateo, it is one of the finest pieces of sculpture in Spain, and a fitting welcome for weary pilgrims. Three doorless arches are intricately carved with Biblical scenes; a superb Last Judgement on the right, and variously interpreted Old Testament scenes on the left. In the centre Santiago himself sits under Christ

Santiago de Compostela

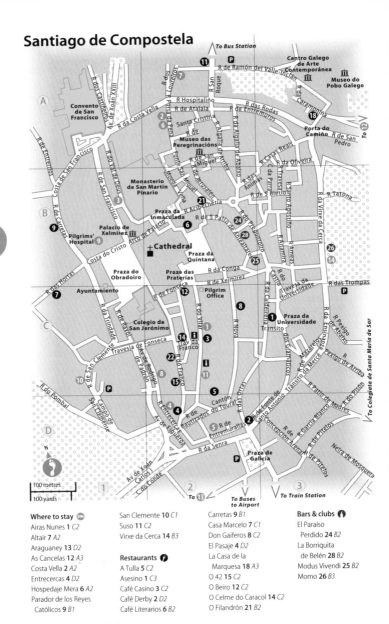

and the Evangelists, who are surrounded by elders of the Apocalypse playing medieval musical instruments.

Upon entering the church, pilgrims queue to touch the pillar by the feet of Santiago; over the centuries five clear finger marks have been worn in the stone. On the other side of the pillar, carved with the Tree of Jesse, many then bump heads with the figure of Master Mateo, hoping that some of his genius will rub off. Many mistakenly butt the head under Santiago's feet; this is in fact Samson; Master Mateo faces into the church.

The interior itself is still attractively Romanesque in the main. High barrel vaulting and the lack of a *coro* in the centre of the nave give an excellent perspective down the church, although it's a pity the original stone *coro* by Master Mateo was destroyed in the early 17th century to make way for a wooden one that is no longer there either (the stone one has been re-assembled in the cathedral museum, the wooden one in the Monasterio de San Martín Pinario).

The massive altar is over-ornate and features some rather out-of-place cherubs on the *baldaquino* (baldachin), which is topped by an image of Santiago in Moor-killing mode; the whole thing belongs on a circus caravan. Above in the cupola is the eye-in-triangle symbol of the all-seeing God. Behind the altar is the image of Santiago himself. Pilgrims ascend behind the statue and give it an *abrazo* (embrace); this, a kiss to the back of his head, and a confession below, was the symbolic end to the pilgrimage.

There are various masses daily, with a special pilgrim one at midday. On occasions during the celebration of mass, a large silver *botafumeiro* (censer) is hung from the ceiling at the crossing and slowly swung by eight men until it covers the whole length of the transept and reaches frightening velocities, diffusing incense and sparks all the while. It's a fantastic and unnerving thing to see, and it's only flown off twice (once in a Mass celebrated for Catherine of Aragón to wish her luck on her journey to wed Henry VIII in England; it was considered a bad omen, as it proved to be). The *botafumeiro* is an expensive thing to light, and is swung only on religious holidays or when a group of pilgrims get €240 together to pay for it. It needs to be reserved at least two days in advance. Contact peregrinos@archicompostela.org.

Cathedral museum
Apr-Oct 0900-2000, Nov-Mar 1000-2000, €6.

Back in the Praza do Obradoiro, investigate the Romanesque **crypt** at the base of the main staircase. One of the three sections of the cathedral museum, it was built by Master Mateo to support the weight of his Romanesque façade above; it's an interesting space dominated by a sturdy load-bearing pillar. There are reproductions of some of the musical instruments that appear on the façade above, as well as some processional crosses and, interestingly, the 14th-century battle-horn of Alfonso XI, made from an elephant's tusk.

The main section of the museum is accessed from the cathedral or the Praza do Obradoiro. Entering from the square, the first rooms contain fragments of Romanesque sculpture, including one of the *Punishment of the Damned*, with two

ON THE ROAD

Rosalía de Castro (1837-1885)

"I do not know what I am seeking, but it is something that I lost I know not when".
Born in Santiago, poet and novelist Rosalía de Castro grew up in Padrón.
Although officially an orphan her mother was, in fact, an unmarried Galician
aristocrat and her father a priest. The publication of her *Cantres Gallegos*
(*Galician songs*) in 1863 is seen as the high-water mark of the Galician
rexurdimento (renewal) movement that sought to express liberal ideas
through the medium of the Galician language.

Her marriage in 1858 to historian and Galician nationalist Manuel Murgula
brought her into contact with other writers who were using the Galician
language to express political ideas. Her main achievement was to express
traditional Galician tales through complex, innovative metre and in her
refreshing use of pastoral imagery. Many of her poems are redolent with
morriña, a particularly Galician word that refers to a melancholy longing;
a feature common to several Atlantic/ Celtic cultures.

Her marriage was not a happy one and for the last years of her life she
struggled with chronic illness. Her ability to find a distinctive voice against
such a difficult background has meant a new interest in her work from
feminist critics. She continues to be a source of inspiration to many Spanish
authors and in Galicia she is a national hero.

naked sinners having their sensitive bits eaten by beasts. The highlight of this section
is the reconstruction of the stone **coro** by Master Mateo, which must have looked
superb in the cathedral until it was destroyed in 1603 to make way for a wooden
one. Some granite slabs elegantly painted in *mudéjar* style are also noteworthy.
Upstairs, there's a range of religious sculpture in both polychrome wood and granite,
including a sensitive San Sebastián in gold shorts and a fine *Last Judgement*, with
an hirsute San Miguel presiding over the psychostasis (weighing of souls). There's
also a wooden relief of the bells of the original church being carried back from
Córdoba, whither they had been taken after Al-Manzur sacked the city. They were
triumphantly reclaimed during the Reconquista, although, underwhelmingly, they
were allegedly found in a pantry, being used to hold olive oil.

The **cloister** is absolutely massive in scale, and has a slightly neglected feel. The
star vaulting is ornate Gothic and the arches heavily elegant. There are several
tombs and fragments around, as well as some large, 18th-century bells. A small
library contains one of the *botafumeiros* (see above), and there are some mediocre
tapestries; but don't despair, there are some better ones upstairs, especially three
depicting the life of Achilles by Rubens.

Between the cloister and the cathedral is the **treasury**, a rather vulgar display of
wealth donated by various bigwigs; the collection includes a goblet that belonged
to Marshal Pétain. Next to this is the **Panteón**, which contains tombs of various kings
of León and other nobles. There's also an immense *retablo* holding the cathedral's

impressive collection of relics; these include the head of the other apostle James, the Lesser (Alpheus), encased in a gilt bust, and a spine from the crown of thorns.

The other section of the museum, on the other side of the cathedral façade, is the **Palacio de Xelmírez**, interesting for being a Romanesque civil building (it was built as an archbishop's residence), although it was heavily modified in the 16th century. Features include an attractive patio and large kitchen and two beautiful halls. This is often given over to temporary exhibitions, which may have an additional charge. There are also guided visits (in Spanish only) available that take you up to the cathedral roof (€12).

Praza de Obradoiro

The other buildings on the Praza do Obradoiro are also interesting. To the left as you face the cathedral is the massive **Pilgrims' Hospital**, built by Fernando and Isabel, the Catholic Monarchs. Now a parador, pilgrims still have the right a free meal here if they are one of the first 10 to queue for 0900, 1200 or 1900 sittings. The hotel has four pretty courtyards named after the evangelists and several elegant halls. Access is limited if you aren't a guest, but the bits you are allowed to wander around are worthwhile.

Opposite the cathedral, the **Ayuntamiento** is housed in an attractive neoclassical building, while the fourth side, opposite the parador, is partly taken up by the **Colegio de San Jerónimo**, a 15th-century structure now part of the university, with a nice little patio and a portal that looks distinctly Romanesque; perhaps the architects didn't want to clash with the Pórtico de la Gloria of the cathedral. Next to it, the **Colegio de Santiago Alfeo** is a Renaissance construction used by the local government.

North of the cathedral

former Benedictine monastery, once the second largest in Spain

Monasterio de San Martín Pinario and around
Tue-Sun 1100-1330, 1600-1830 summer 1030-1330, 1600-1900, €2.50.

North of the cathedral, the San Martín Pinario mona**stery** is half restricted to students, but you can enter the church and museum from the back. The door is high and rather overbearing; it's reached via an attractive downward staircase. The interior is lofty and bare, with a massive dome. In contrast to the sober architectural lines is the huge altarpiece, described by the 19th-century traveller Richard Ford: "In the *retablo*, of vilest Churrigueresque, Santiago and San Martín ride together in a fricasee of gilt gingerbread."

Similarly decorative *retablos* adorn the side chapels. Of more interest is the *coro* behind the altar; see if you can find the hidden door that the monks used to enter through. The museum has some old printing presses, an interesting old pharmacy and the wooden choir from the cathedral. There's also a multimedia exhibition on Galicia.

Convento de San Francisco
Near to the monastery is the Convento de San Francisco, founded by Saint Francis when he made the pilgrimage here in the early 13th century, and the **Museo das Peregrinacións** ⓘ *www.mdperegrinacions.com, Tue-Sat 1000-1400, 1600-*

ON THE ROAD

Saint James and the Camino de Santiago

The patron saint of Spain is one of the most revered of figures in the country. St James, or Santiago, was the son of Zebedee, brother of the apostle John, and a fisherman who gave up his nets to follow Christ. In AD 44 he was martyred at swordpoint by King Herod Agrippa. Several centuries later, a small west European kingdom flexing its Christian muscles was in need of a holy warrior.

We move to Galicia, and a spot near the end of the world, Finisterre. In the early ninth century, 800 years after James was martyred and thousands of miles away, a shepherd was guided by an angel and stars to a tomb in the woods at a place now called Compostela. The local bishop, evidently not a man to reserve judgement, deemed it to be St James himself. The news spread fast, and gave the Christians new faith for their fight against the Moors. Even handier than faith on a muddy battlefield is a back-from-the-dead apostle on a white charger, and Santiago obliged. He brutally slew hundreds of hapless Muslims in battle, winning himself the nickname Matamoros, or slayer of Moors.

All very well, but how and why was his body in Spain in the first place? He had, after all, been killed in Caesarea. But tradition, however historically debatable, has it that he preached in Spain at some point, and the Virgin Mary is said to have appeared to him in Zaragoza (at the time called Caesarea too; a possible source of the confusion). James went back to the Holy Land with a few keen Spanish converts. After his death the followers rescued his body and set forth for home with it. Not experts in boat buying, they selected a stone yacht, but with the saint on board, they managed to navigate it to the Pillars of Hercules and around to Galicia. Along the way, the saint performed a miracle, saving a gentleman whose panicked horse had dashed headlong into the sea with him in the saddle. Man and horse rose from the seabed safe and sound; some traditions hold that they were covered in scallop shells; this became the apostle's symbol. His followers landed near Padrón and requested oxen from the local pagan queen so that they could transport the body inland. In mockery, she gave them a pair of ferocious bulls, but the apostle intervened and transformed them into docile

2000 (1700-2100 summer), Sun 1100-1400, €2.50, a three-floor display about the pilgrimage to Santiago, images and iconography of the saint, the Pórtico de la Gloria, and the medieval life of the town. It's reasonably interesting, more so if you're a pilgrim, but ducks a few crucial Saint James issues.

Around Porta do Camino
a lovely area at the pilgrims' entrance to the city

At the eastern end of town, opposite the Porta do Camino where pilgrims enter the city, are two more museums.

beasts, thus converting the amazed queen. After the long journey, Santiago's loyal companions buried him and he was conveniently forgotten until the shepherd's discovery centuries later.

The pilgrims News that an apostle's tomb was in Christian Galicia travelled fast. A church was built and granted a perpetual *voto*, a tax payable by every inhabitant of Spain; this was levied until the 19th century. Pilgrims began to make the journey to Galicia to venerate the saint's remains. Most of the early pilgrims were from France, and the main route across Northern Spain came to be known as the Camino Francés. Waystations for pilgrims were set up, and French settlers and monks became a significant presence in the towns and villages along the route, and continued to be so; many of the churches and cathedrals are based on models from France. In the 12th century a French monk, Aimery Picaud, wrote the *Codex Calixtinus*, part of which was an entertaining guidebook for pilgrims making the journey to Santiago; the dangers mentioned include robbers, con-artists and wolves.

The pilgrimage became phenomenally popular, helped along by the Pope's declaration that all pilgrims to Santiago would have their time in Purgatory halved; if they went on a Holy Year (when the feast of St James, 25 July, falls on a Sunday) they would get a full remission (plenary indulgence). They came from all over Europe; some by boat (Chaucer's Wife of Bath made the journey), some walking for more than a year. At its peak, some half a million pilgrims arrived annually in Santiago, which rapidly became a flourishing city.

The pilgrimage declined in the 19th century, although there was a brief revival when the bones of Santiago, missing for a couple of centuries, were rediscovered (it was proved because a fragment of St James's skull from Pistoia in Italy fit exactly into a handy notch in the Compostela skull) and by the mid-20th century only a handful of people were following the route, whose pilgrim hostels had long since disappeared.

However, in the late 20th century there was a surprising revival in the pilgrimage, whose popularity has continued to grow. Well over 100,000 pilgrims arrive in Santiago on foot and bicycle every year, many more in Holy Years (the next is 2021).

The **Museo do Pobo Galego** ⓘ *T981 583 620, www.museodopobo.es, Tue-Sat 1030-1400, 1600-1930, Sun 1100-1400, €3*, was originally founded by Saint Dominic as a monastery. Inside is a monumental cloister and many ethnographic exhibits relating to Galician life. It's worth a look just for the architecture, including a stunning spiral staircase. There's also a chapel where the poet Rosalía de Castro is buried. Next to the museum, the **Centro Galego de Arte Contemporánea** ⓘ *www.cgac.org, Tue-Sun 1100-2000, free*, is a modern building whose attractive white spaces provide a break from the timeworn granite. Exhibitions are of a high international standard; check their website for what's on. There's also a bookshop and café.

Colegiata de Santa María de Sar

the leaning pillars create a peculiar and impressive beauty

The Colegiata de Santa María de Sar is a Romanesque church a 15-minute walk south of the centre. Built in the 12th century, on insecure ground, it is remarkable chiefly for the alarming lean of its interior columns; after the Lisbon earthquake of 1755, massive buttresses had to be added.

There's a small **museum** ⓘ *www.colegiatadesar.com, Mon-Sat 1000-1300, 1600-1900, €1*, with a tiny bit of Saint Peter in a reliquary, and a cloister, of which one side survives with carvings attributed to Master Mateo. To get there from the Rúa Fonte de San Antonio off Praza de Galicia, take the second right down Rúa Patio de Madres and follow it down the hill; the church is on your right after the railway bridge.

Listings Santiago de Compostela *map p24*

Tourist information

Galicia's tourist board, **Turgalicia**, publishes useful booklets and brochures. The website, www. turgalicia.es, is also worth a browse. Santiago has several tourist information offices, including one at the airport. The most useful are listed below.

Galician regional office
Rúa do Vilar 30, T981 584 081, www. turgalicia.es. Mon-Fri 1000-2000, Sat 1100-1400, 1700-1900, Sun 1100-1400 .

Municipal office
Rúa do Vilar 63, T981 555 129, www. santiagoturismo.com. Winter Mon-Fri 0900-1900, Sat-Sun 0900-1400, 1600-1900, summer daily 0900-2100.

Pilgrim office
Rúa do Vilar 1, around the corner from the cathedral, T981 568 846, www. peregrinossantiago.es. Easter-Oct 0900-2100, Nov-Easter Mon-Sat 1000-2000, Sun 1000-1400, 1600-2000.
The place to get your pilgrim passport stamped.

Where to stay

There are well over 100 places to stay in Santiago, with plenty in the budget range to cater for the pilgrim traffic. Many restaurants in the centre have a few cheap rooms too. Rooms can be hard to find in summer, but it's just a matter of persistence.

€€€€ Hotel Araguaney
C Alfredo Brañas 5, T981 559 600, www.araguaney.com.
Not in the old town, but not far from Praza Galicia, this hotel has rather bland decor but makes up for it with good service, and plenty of space, comfort and facilities in the rooms. There's also a high-quality restaurant. You can often get much lower rates through travel agents or online discounters.

€€€€ Parador de los Reyes Católicos
Praza do Obradoiro 1, T981 582 200, www.parador.es.
Although these days it's beyond the budgets of many 21st-century peregrines, the pilgrims' hostel built by the Catholic monarchs is a luxurious place to lie up and is by far the city's

most atmospheric place to stay. Built around 4 beautiful courtyards, it's worth splashing out for the history and location alone. It's on the cathedral square, and the rooms lack nothing of the class of the building.

€€€ Hotel Altaïr
Rúa dos Loureiros 12, T981 554 712, www.altairhotel.net.
Modern, effortlessly attractive and stylish, this boutique hotel blends warm minimalism in the superbly comfortable rooms with exposed stone reflecting the centre of historic Santiago. Attentive staff and tasty breakfasts set you up perfectly for getting to know Compostela. Recommended.

€€€ Virxe da Cerca
Rúa Virxe da Cerca 27, T981 569 350, www.pousadasdecompostela.com.
This lovely old stone building on the road circling Santiago's old town has been converted into this stylish and characterful hotel. While the rooms are as well equipped as in any big hotel, there's a more enchanting feel here, particularly around the delightful central patio. Rooms in the historic section are slightly dearer. Recommended.

€€ Costa Vella
Porta da Peña 17, T981 569 530, www.costavella.com.
This smart, comfortable hotel is one of the best in this price range. It's got a romantic feel, not least for its fantastic garden studded with apple and lemon trees and offering fantastic views. Some of the rooms overlook it (they are slightly more expensive); the interior decor is stylish and beautiful, and the welcome from the owners is genuine. Highly recommended.

€€ Hotel Airas Nunes
Rúa do Vilar 17, T981 569 350, www.pousadasdecompostela.com.
Right in the thick of things, this modern and stylish hotel has excellent facilities and plenty of attractive charm in a 17th-century building. Rooms are on the small side but comfortable and the location is hard to better. Bottom end of this price category.

€€ Hotel Entrecercas
Rúa Entrecercas 11, T981 571 151, www.entrecercas.es.
A charming little hotel that's central but tucked away from the busier parts. It has charm as well as courteous and helpful management. Breakfast included. Underground parking close by. Recommended.

€€ Hotel San Clemente
Rúa San Clemente 28, T981 569 260, www.pousadasdecompostela.com.
An excellent option located in the old town below and close to the cathedral. The charm of the old house still shines through, but the rooms are equipped to modern standards with good if small bathrooms and free Wi-Fi.

€ Hospedaje Mera
Porta da Pena 15, T981 583 867, www.hospedajemera.com.
This quiet and cheap option is on a pedestrian street in the centre of town. Facilities are basic – there are rooms with and without bathroom available – but some rooms have balconies and views, and it's in a great location.

€ Suso
Rúa Vilar 65, T981 586 611, www.hostalsuso.com.
This central pilgrims' favourite is handy for everything in town. Its spacious (not the singles), en suite rooms are

very good value year-round (it's worth getting here early to avoid disappointment) and there's a friendly vibe from management and the happy walkers at journey's end (unlike the pilgrims of yesteryear, they don't have to turn around and walk back home again). Highly recommended.

Camping

As Cancelas
T981 580 266, www.camping ascancelas.com. Open year-round.
A good campsite within 30 mins' walk of the heart of town, and frequently served by city bus No 9. There are various family-sized bungalows as well as a shop and a pool.

Ciudad de Vacaciones Monte do Gozo
Ctra Aeropuerto s/n, T981 558 942, www.cvacaciones-montedogozo.com.
A massive summer-only campsite and holiday village on the hill 2 km east of town with regular public transport and all facilities, including a pool.

Restaurants

Seafood is the thing to eat in Santiago, as indeed in much of Galicia. One of the main streets, Rúa Franco, is something of a tourist trap (although locals eat here too); prices are high and quality variable. *Vieiras* (scallops) are an obvious choice, served in a bacon and onion sauce, but they're expensive at about €6 each. *Percebes* are also popular, as are *cigalas* (a word to the wise: *cigalas* are expensive and menus often somewhat misleadingly list the price per 100 g; 6 chubby *cigalas* can weigh well over 500 g). *Tarta de Santiago* is an almond cake often engraved with a sword; patisseries

along Rúa Franco give out free morsels to taste.

€€€ Carretas
C Carretas 21, T981 563 111, www. restaurancesanclemente.com.
Excellent fish and meat dishes are to be had in this high-quality straight-down-the-line Galician restaurant. Service is excellent and the location just below the cathedral square very central. Recommended.

€€€ Casa Marcelo
Rúa das Hortas 3, T981 558 850, www.casamarcelo.net. Tue-Sat.
This little gourmet's paradise is on one of Santiago's most picturesque streets just below the Praza do Obradoiro. You won't spend hours browsing the menu, for it's *table d'hôte* only. The feast on offer changes daily, but consists of 5-6 courses full of delicate flavours for €65. Delicate dishes are an intriguing blend of Japanese and local influences and are all delicious. Diners all sit at one sociable table. Recommended.

€€€ Don Gaiferos
Rúa Nova 23, T981 583 894, www.dongaiferos.com.
A dark and moody but modernized place that offers plenty of choice of the finest Galician produce in a good location close to the cathedral. Excellent daily seafood specials, but you might also be tempted by the meat on offer; the *tournedos* are delicious, and the steak tartare just as it should be. Mains are €17-25, and there's a degustation menu.

€€€ El Pasaje
Rúa Franco 54, T981 557 081, www.restaurantepasaje.com.
A class above the other fish restaurants on this street, this is at the open end near the Alameda and has room for 3 or 4

outdoor tables. The seafood is sublime, though extremely expensive. The fish cooked *a la parrilla* is memorable, and there's a fine range of wine to accompany it. The *zamburiñas* (mini-scallops) make a fine appetizer. Be aware of the price/weight equation.

€€ Asesino
Praza Universidad 16, T981 581 568.
Discreetly signposted, this restaurant opposite the university is a long-standing Santiago classic that opens when it chooses, and offers excellent home-style food accompanied by appropriately familiar bric-a-brac decor. Almost everything is worthwhile, but the *navajas* (razor shells) are particularly succulent.

€€ La Casa de la Marquesa
Costa de San Domingos 2, T981 573 958, www.lacasade lamarquesa.es.
Nicely positioned near the modern art gallery, and with an appealing terrace with outdoor tables, this place is frequented by smart young Santiago folk and offers upmarket meals and tapas, as well as creditable sushi twice a week.

€€ O 42
Rúa Franco 42, T981 581 009, www.restauranteo42.com.
This place on the main eat street certainly doesn't try to curry favour with pilgrims or tourists except through being authentic. The seafood is slightly pricier than at neighbouring places, but it's top quality, especially the octopus and *navajas* (razor clams). Sit at the rustic wooden tables to enjoy the traditional Santiago *raciones*.

€€ O Beiro
Rúa da Raíña 3, T981 581 370.
Stocked with hundreds of wines from all over Spain, this is the place for an impromptu tasting session. The shop has an atmospheric back bar, with flagstones and a low wood-beamed ceiling, where you can try several of their wines by the glass or any of them (and there's over a 1000) by the bottle. There's a free tapa with every glass, and other local produce for sale. Recommended.

€€ O Celme do Caracol
C Raíña 22, T981 571 746, www.ocelmedocaracol.com.
Abuzz with upbeat Galician chat, this happy place with a sustainable bent a few paces from the cathedral turns out truly delicious bistro-style Galician fare in its intimate 2-level space. Downstairs, the bar pours good wines by the glass, and complements them with generous free tapas from the semi-open kitchen. Find a table, and enjoy a marvellous seafood soup, top salads, and, as the name suggests, snails in a spicy sauce. Prices are more than fair.

€ A Tulla
Ruela de Entreruas 1, T981 580 889, www.restauranteatulla.net.
In a tiny square reached by the narrowest of passageways, this secluded, rustic, and enchanting spot looks like Grandma's house and does simple, delicious old-style Galician cooking from an open kitchen. There's a great vegetarian set menu as well. Recommended.

€ O Filandón
C Azabachería 6, T981 572 378.
This cosy wine bar is popular with arriving pilgrims, whose messages on paper serviettes adorn the walls. There's an excellent atmosphere and very good service from the personable boss.

Cafés
There's nowhere better in town for a relaxing outdoor drink than the garden

of the **Costa Vella** hotel (see Where to stay, above).

Café Casino
Rúa do Vilar 35, T981 577 503, www.cafecasino.es.
This historic café is awash with 19th-century plushness. It's a massive space, beautiful, elegant and popular with young and old for evening coffee.

Café Derby
C Huérfanas 29, T981 586 417, www.cafederby.com.
Over 80 years old, this noble old café seems to have changed little, and it's much the better for it. Polite service, cosy worn seating, cut-glass chandeliers, and plenty of space make it a Santiago classic.

Café Literarios
Praza Quintana 1, T981 565 630.
A great spot on this attractive and unusual square, named after the redoubtable student batallion of this granite city. It's still got an arty feel inside, while the terrace gazes over the architectural glories of the old centre.

Bars and clubs

The student nightlife kicks off around Rúa Nova de Abaixos near Praza Roxa. Get the free newspaper *Compostelán* or *7 Días Santiago* for bar, club events and other venue listings.

El Paraíso Perdido
Rúa San Paio de Antealtares 3.
This basement bar has an intriguing 'hell gate' entrance. Inside it's decorated with mosaics, and there's a chilled-out, buzzy, hippy-trippy atmosphere.

La Borriquita de Belén
Rúa San Paio de Antealtares 22.
A sociable and lively bar tucked away behind the cathedral and playing host to regular live jazz and traditionally influenced Galician bands.

Modus Vivendi
Praza Feijóo 1, T981 576 109, www.pubmodusvivendi.net.
Once a stable, you can still use the old horse trough as a table. The stone arches lend a medieval ambience to what is one of Santiago's friendliest and most characterful drinking options. Recommended.

Momo
Rúa da Virxe da Cerca 23, www.pubmomo.com.
This massive bar on the edge of the old town comes equipped with its own street and zebra crossing. In summer the terrace opens – it's a fantastic spot to be, with great views.

Entertainment

Check the website www.compostela cultura.org for upcoming concerts and events.
Auditorio de Galicia, *T981 552 290, www.auditoriodegalicia.org*. North of town. Classical concerts and opera.

Festivals

25 Jul Santiago's main fiesta is the day of the **St James** himself. When this day falls on a Sun, it's known as a **Holy Year** (the next one is 2021). Apart from partying, there's a solemn Mass and a spectacular pyrotechnic display the night before.

Shopping

Bookshops
Librería Universitas (Rúa Fernando III el Santo 3, T981 592 438); **Librería San Pablo** (Rúa do Vilar 37, T981 552 180).

Food and drink
The **Mercado de Abastos** is a lively food market in the old town on Praza de Abastos. **O Beiro** (Rúa da Raíña 3, www.obeiro.com), is a good place to buy (as well as drink) Galician and other Spanish wines.

Gems
Santiago is a good place to purchase *azabache* (jet), but beware of vendors near the cathedral who make a living preying on tourists.

Transport
Buy a copy of the newspaper *El Correo Gallego* for a complete list of transport times.

Air
Santiago de Compostela Airport (SCQ), is 11 km east of town in Lavacolla. Buses run from the airport to the the bus station via the centre (€3). It's €20 in a cab. **Ryanair** flies to London Stansted, Frankfurt Hahn and Milan Bergamo, as well as Madrid and several other Spanish airports. **Vueling** fly direct to Paris and Barcelona, while **Easyjet** serve London Gatwick, Geneva and Basel and **Aer Lingus**, Dublin.

Buses connect the airport with the city centre and bus station, stopping at the corner of Av Xeneral Pardiñas and Rúa da República de El Salvador; they run approximately hourly (€3).

Bus
The bus station is a 20-min walk northeast of the centre. Bus Nos 5 and C5 run there from Praza de Galicia via Rúa da Virxe da Cerca. If arriving by bus, head up the hill directly opposite the bus station café and turn left at the big intersection.

Within Galicia, buses run hourly to **A Coruña** (via motorway 45 mins, via road 1 hr 20 mins), 3 a day to **Fisterra** and **Camariñas**. 8 buses to **Lugo**, hourly ones to **Pontevedra** (45 mins) and **Vigo**, and 7 to **Ourense**. Buses run hourly to **Ribeira**, and 6 times a day to **Vilagarcía**, **Cambados** and **O Grove**.

Services connect with **Bilbao** (3 daily, 12 hrs), **Ponferrada** (5 daily, 3½-4 hrs), **Madrid** (5-6 daily, 8-9 hrs), **Oviedo** (5 a day, 5 hrs 30 mins) and **Gijón**, and **Salamanca** (2 daily, 6 hrs 15 mins) via **Zamora**, among other destinations.

Car hire
Autos Brea, C Gómez Ulla 10, T981 562 670, www.autosbrea.com, is reasonably central. There are also several multinationals at the airport.

Train
The train station is south of the centre, about a 15-min walk down Rúa de Hórreo (off Praza Galicia). Trains run regularly to **A Coruña** (45 mins, €7), **Vigo** (1 hr 20 mins, from €9), and **Ourense** (4 a day, 1 hr 30 mins, €19); there's also a sleeper and a day train to **Madrid** (9½ hrs and 5¾ hrs respectively, €51-55).

Rías Altas

The north coast of Galicia, not as overdeveloped as the west coast, has some interesting fishing towns and a few cracking beaches. The inlets of the Rías Altas are deep, making perfect natural harbours and sheltered (if chilly) swimming spots. Of the two major ports on the north coast, Ferrol is an earthy industrial centre, while A Coruña is a jewel set on a promontory with a harbour on one side, a great beach on the other and a lively seafood tapas scene. For cliffscapes, Garita de Herbeira is hard to beat.

Ribadeo

lively port town with spectacular rock arches nearby

Ribadeo faces its Asturian counterpart Castropol across the broad expanse of the inlet at the mouth of the river Eo; thus the town's name. It's a functional but pleasant enough place, with a waterside promenade by the harbour at the bottom of the steep streets leading down from the old centre, which is centred on the Praza de Espanha with its ornate turn-of-the-20th century buildings. The views across to Asturias a mile away across the water are picturesque, and the modern bridge over the *ría* are impressive, despite the thundering traffic. Past the bridge there's the small Forte de San Damián, built to protect the town from seaward invasion. The old centre is pleasant too, with a good square with plenty of palm trees. There are many *indiano* houses, attractive structures built by Galicians returned from the Americas.

West of Ribadeo

Along this first stretch of Galician coast are some of the region's best **beaches**, all within a 20-minute walk of the main road. **As Catedrais** (the cathedrals) is a pretty little stretch named for its spectacularly eroded cliffs and rocks lying in the water. It all but disappears at high tide. Nearby **Reinante** is a superb length of whitish sand, as is **Arealonga**, while a little further, **Praia de Lóngara** and adjacent Fontela are the best options for surfing.

Tourist information

Ribadeo Tourist Office
*On the square in the old centre,
T982 128 689, turismo@ribadeo.org.
Mon-Fri 1030-1400, 1600-1900, Sat 1030-
1400, 1600-2000, Sun 1030-1400.*

Where to stay

€€€ Parador de Ribadeo
*Rúa Amador Fernández 7, T982 128 825,
www.parador.es.*
The town's best place to stay, this
parador is not the most characterful of
its kind but has views across the *ría* and
a reasonable seafood restaurant. It feels
about due for a renovation.

€€ Hotel Mediante
*Praza de Espanha 8, T982 130 453,
www.hotelmediante.com.*
Nicely placed in the middle of the old
town, where the main pedestrian street
meets the square, this welcoming family-
run hotel has spacious, simple, en suite
rooms with chessboard tiling. It's an
absolute bargain (€) off-season. There's
also a café-restaurant. Recommended.

Camping

There are several campsites to the west
of town, including **Ribadeo** (2 km from
Ribadeo, T982 131 167, www.camping
ribadeo.com), which boasts a pool and
has bungalows. Open Easter and Jun-Sep.

West of Ribadeo

€€ Casa Guillermo
*Vista Alegre 3, Santiago de
Reinante, Barreiros, T982 134 150,
www.casaguillermo.net.*

A good place to stay if you've got kids;
it's near to the beach and has a large
garden and spotless, attractive, and
comfortable rooms. The hosts are
welcoming and it's open year-round.

€€ Hotel A Finca
*Rúa Playa 14, Barreiros, T982 124 611,
www.hotelafinca.com.*
Easily accessed and well located for
exploration of the best beaches along
this coast, this upbeat, cheery place has
extra-friendly owners, a tasty breakfast
(included) and a relaxing garden.

Camping

A Nosa Casa
*by Reinante beach, T982 134 065,
www.campinganosacasa.com.*
One of several campsites in this stretch,
Nosa Casa is open year-round and also
has hotel accommodation (€€) and
1- or 2-room bungalows.

Restaurants

€€ Solana
C Antonio Otero 41, T982 128 835.
This is a reliably good seafood restaurant
by the marina. Anything from the water
is delicious, but the paella or *zarzuela
de mariscos* (seafood stew) are excellent
house specialities. Recommended.

€ Casa Villaronta
Rúa San Francisco 9, T982 128 609.
Down the pedestrian street from the
central square, this is a downmarket
and delightfully traditional Galician
pulpería, where *ribeiro* wine and a plate
of octopus is the way to go. It's always
packed, and the low prices are only part
of the reason why.

What to do

At Ribadeo's waterfront you can practise or learn various aquatic activities.

¡Hola!Ola, *Av Calvo Sotelo 30, T982 120 064, www.holaola.com.* Offer hire of surf equipment and lessons, and also deal in waterskiing, wakeboarding and windsurfing.
Portanorte, *Av Asturias 21, T982 120 429, www.portanorte.es.* Boat-oriented and hire kayaks, yachts and hobby catamarans.

Bus
8 buses daily to **Lugo**, 7 along the coast to **Oviedo**, 4 to **Santiago**, and several running to **A Coruña** along the coast. 2 buses head inland to **Vilalba** and **Mondoñedo**.

Train
The coastal **FEVE** train line stops here on its way between **Ferrol** and **Oviedo**. It's a good way to access some smaller coastal towns.

Foz and around

low-key but friendly town with an interesting church to visit

The best feature of Foz is its attractive working fishing port, where the fishermen's families come down to wave at the boats heading out to sea. The rest of the town is friendly but not particularly interesting.

A good excursion is the walk or drive to **San Martín de Mondoñedo**, a hamlet whose **church** ① *Tue-Sun 1100-1400, 1600-1800 (the keyholder lives nearby)*, was once a cathedral; the bishop must have been the least stressed of primates. It's about 8 km from town along a pleasant road heavy with the scent of eucalypts. Although the church's origins are ninth century, most of what is visible is later Romanesque. It's on soft ground and is heavily buttressed; the apse has Lombard arching, a feature of the Romanesque of Catalunya. There's an attractive *cruceiro* outside, and the portal features the Lamb. Inside are some excellent Romanesque wallpaintings, good carved capitals and the tomb of Gonzalo, yet another Galician saint.

West of Foz

Moving westwards, the coast becomes a little more rugged, but there are still some decent beaches tucked into coves. As well, a multitude of rivers flow down to the sea from the Galician high country and are good spots for trout fishing. The straggling village of **Xove** is less impressive than its name, which derives from the Latin *Iovii*, meaning 'of Jupiter'.

Few places appeal as a stopover until you reach the **Ría de Viveiro**. Near the town of Celeiro is the excellent patrolled beach of **Area**, a duney stretch that looks across to an islet.

Where to stay

€€ Isla Nova Hotel
Rúa Emilia Pardo Bazán 7, T982 133 606,
www.islanovahotel.es.
Welcoming and modern, this central
Foz hotel is close to the beach and has
good-value compact rooms, some with
sea views.

Restaurants

€ Restaurante O Lar
Praza Conde Fontao 3, Foz, T982 140 829.
This place is a good, traditional and solid
harbourside eatery with reliable and
cheap seafood.

Viveiro and around

well-preserved historic town famous for its Easter festival

Viveiro is a friendly and interesting little place that makes the best stop on
this stretch of coast. Right at the tail of the *ría*, its small boats get marooned
on mudflats at low tide. Viveiro is reasonably lively in summer, when there's
a small but steady flow of holidaymakers, but it's very quiet for the rest of the
year. The town is within easy range of many fine beaches, including Area (see
above). Viveiro is particularly known for its Easter festival, a serious event with
a candlelit procession enacting the stations of the cross, and the town also
pushes the boat out at Christmas with a marvellous life-size Nativity scene
surrounding the church.

The old town is interesting, and preserves fragments of its walls as well as a few
gates, one a very tight squeeze at the top of the town. Built in the 12th century,
the Romanesque **Iglesia de Santa María del Campo** is in the centre of the old
town. Inside is a pretty processional cross dating from the 16th century, as well as
a sculptural assembly that used to adorn one of the gates of the town wall. Nearby
is a replica of the grotto at Lourdes; locals seem to trust it; there's many an offering
of plastic body parts, soliciting intervention for physical ailments.

Around Viveiro

The coastline continues in rugged vein after Viveiro; as the road ascends the
western headland there are some excellent views over the *ría* and out to sea.
The small fishing village of **O Barqueiro** is a peaceful spot to stay, although the
roadside sprawl above isn't so attractive. There's a bank in town, and a choice of
places to stay on the small harbour. Just east of here, the lovely sandy crescent of
Arealonga beach is one of the best in the vicinity.

From here, it's an hour's walk through eucalypt forest to **Punto Estaca de
Bares**, the northernmost point in Spain. A winding road leads up to a viewpoint
(signposted *Semáforo*; the signal station has now been converted into a stunning
rural hotel, see Where to stay, page 40), while at the cape itself is a lighthouse

and whipping winds. There are some shops in the village, a good restaurant and a superb sandy beach a mile long and sheltered by a reef that was probably built by the Phoenicians.

Tourist information

Municipal tourist office
Av Ramón Canosa s/n, on the roundabout near the centre of town, T982 560 879, www.viveiro.es. Sep-Jun Mon-Fri 1100-1400, 1630-1930, Sat 1100-1400, 1700-1900, Jul-Aug Mon-Fri 1000-1400, 1630-2000, Sat 1100-1400, 1700-1900, Sun 1130-1330.

The large **Centro Comarcal** *(Mon-Fri 1000-1430, 1700-2000)*, nearby, also has tourist information.

Where to stay

As well as the options below, there are a couple of intriguing *casas rurales* in noble historic buildings within a short distance of Viveiro: the **€€ Casa da Torre** (Toxeiras 47, Landrove, T982 598 026, www.casadatorreviveiro.com), and upmarket **€€€ Pazo da Trave** (Trave, T982 598 163, www.pazodatrave.com).

€€€ Hotel Ego
Playa de Area s/n, T982 560 987, www.hotelego.com.
East of Viveiro, this hotel has an excellent situation above Area beach. It's a relaxed and well-equipped hotel for stress-free summer holidays. The terrace and most rooms boast excellent views over the strand and *ría*, and there's a pool and good restaurant. Recommended.

€€ Hostal O Forno
O Barqueiro, T981 414 124, www.hostaloforno.com.

This is a great little place to stay, lovingly renovated and cared for; it looks over the water and also has a good seafood restaurant.

€€ Hotel Orfeo
Av García Navia Castrillón 2, Viveiro, T982 562 101, www.hotel-orfeo.com.
Showing its age a little these days, this is well located on the water in Viveiro itself. Many of the comfortable rooms come with a balcony and a view at no extra cost. It drops down to € off season. Free Wi-Fi.

€€ Hotel Semáforo de Bares
O Barqueiro s/n, T981 417 147, www.hotelsemaforodebares.com.
The signal station at the Bares cape has been intriguingly converted into a place to stay. Though it's Spain's most northerly hotel, it doesn't need to rely on geographical quirks: the location is stunning, and the rooms, of which there are a variety, are great. Cosy little doubles under the sloping roof are the most economical. Best though, is the suite (€€€), formerly the control room for monitoring marine traffic; a marvellous hexagonal space with windows all around. There's a restaurant and a good welcome. Recommended.

€ Fonda Nuevo Mundo
Rúa Teodoro de Quirós 14, Viveiro, T982 560 025.
At the upper end of town, this is a good, friendly budget option if you don't mind the sound of church bells.

Camping

Camping Viveiro
Playa de Covas s/n, T982 560 004.
Open late Jun-Sep.
Across the estuary from the heart of
town and on a popular patrolled beach
with greyish sand.

Restaurants

The restaurant at the **Hotel Ego**
(see Where to stay, above) has a
lofty reputation for seafood.

€€ O Asador
Rúa Meliton Cortiñas 15, T982 560 688.
This is the most inviting restaurant in
Viveiro itself, a friendly upstairs spot
looking over the narrow lane below. The
fish, octopus and service are superb.
Recommended.

€€ Vinoteca Los Leones
Pastor Díaz 12, T982 570 604.
In a shopping arcade between the
waterfront and the main pedestrian
street, this smart little bar serves quality
wines in pretty glasses and also does
a few smart food options like *pirulís de
perdiz*, a little partridge-meat flourish.

€ Mesón Imperial
Pastor Díaz 66, T982 562 316.
Reliably buzzing at afternoon tapas time,
this is a traditional tasca with a struggle
to get to the bar, and delicious *raciones*
like mussels, monkfish brochettes, and,
of course, octopus.

What to do

If you fancy a bit of boating, you can
rent canoes on the Praia de Covas
beach just across the *ría* from town.
Roq Sport, *T646 514 602, www.roqsport.
com*. Land-based activities including
guided hikes, mountain biking, kayaking
and abseiling.

Transport

Bus
Buses run from here both ways along the
coast and inland to **Lugo** and **Santiago**.
The bus station is by the water 200 m
north of the old town.

Train
The **FEVE** line stops at Viveiro, and also
at O Barqueiro near the main road,
as do buses on the coastal road.

Ortigueira and around

incredible views over dramatic cliffscapes

The town of Ortigueira is a fairly workaday fishing port, transformed in mid-July
for a massive festival of Celtic music and culture (www.festivaldeortigueira.com).
Otherwise, there's no real reason to stop here; a quick look at its gardened port
will suffice. A short distance west of Ortigueira, the main road cuts inland, but
it's worth exploring the headland, a wild and rugged landscape battered by
some of Galicia's worst weather. Apart from the dull sprawl of Carriño, it's a bleak
and lonely place populated mainly by wild horses. North of Carriño, the pretty
Cabo Ortegal has a lighthouse and good views; it's a nice walk along the green
clifftops. Further west, the Garita de Herbeira is an atmospheric and desolate
arch of high granite cliffs 600 m high, and pounded by waves and weather.

Further west, the **Santuario de San Andrés de Teixido** is in a sturdy stone hamlet. It's a simple chapel that was established by the Knights of Malta, who brought a relic of Saint Andrew here back from the Holy Land. The saint is much venerated along this understandably superstitious coast, and there's always a good pile of *ex voto* offerings that range from representations of what intervention is being sought for, such as models of fishing boats or plastic body parts to simple gifts of pens and cigarettes. There's a well-attended *romería* (pilgrimage procession) to the sanctuary on 8 September; some of the pilgrims make the journey in coffins to give thanks for narrow escapes, mostly at sea.

Listings Ortigueira and around

Where to stay

€€ Río da Cruz
In the middle of the headland, some 9 km inland from Garita de Herbeira, T981 428 057, www.riodacruz.com.

A lovely old stone farmhouse with cosy pinewood rooms, one of which is an appealing duplex that costs a little more. They serve pleasant meals, which can be eaten on an outdoor terrace.

Cedeira and around

wild rugged coastline popular for surfing

South of the sanctuary of San Andrés de Teixido, and back on the main road is Cedeira, a pleasant town on yet another picturesque *ría*. There are some excellent beaches around, although the town beach isn't the best of them; try A Magdalena, a shallow-watered strip of sand a couple of kilometres further along the coast. The two halves of Cedeira are linked by a bridge; the old town is across it from the main road, and is a warren of steep and narrow streets.

Cedeira coastline

West of Cedeira is some of the nicest coastline in these parts, heavily wooded and studded with excellent beaches, particularly **Villarube** and **Do Rodo**, one of Galicia's best surf beaches. **Da Frouxeira** is another excellent strip of sand, 2.5 km long, and backed by a lagoon that is an important haven for waterfowl. There's a good (if slightly pricey) campsite at **Valdoviño**, on the main road near Da Frouxeira beach. There's a simpler campsite near the Praia do Río, which also has good surf (see Where to stay, opposite). Buses are the only way to access the coast on public transport, as the FEVE line has cut inland by this point.

Where to stay

€ Chelsea
Praza Sagrado Corazón 10, T981 482 340,
www.hostalchelsea.com.
This is an acceptable place on a nice
square very near the beach, across the
bridge from the main part of town.

Cedeira coastline
Camping

Fontesín
Near the Praia do Río, T981 485 028,
www.campingfontesin.com.
Jun to mid-Sep only.
Simpler than the one at Valdoviño,
but also has good surf.

Valdoviño
On the main road near Da
Frouxeira beach, T981 487 076,
www.turvaldovino.com. Easter-Sep.
A good (if slightly pricey) campsite,
it has bungalows and many facilities.

Restaurants

€€ Badulaque
C Area Longa 1, T981 492 265.
This local sits near the port in the
Casa do Mar building. It's an old-
fashioned sort of a place that does
seafood and fish with few frills but
of a very high standard.

Ferrol

earthy industrial centre with an interesting waterfront

While Ferrol's glory days as a naval harbour ended abruptly (along with most of Spain's fleet) during the Peninsular War, it's still an important port, and the navy is very much in evidence. Although poor and with high unemployment, Ferrol has not been shorn of its dignity; the streets around the harbour are lined with noble terraced houses, and locals are proud of their city and its hardworking heritage. Perhaps Ferrol's greatest claim to fame, however, is seldom mentioned these days: in the winter of 1892 an uptight little boy was born to a naval family in a house near the harbour. Francisco Franco y Bahamonde went on to rule Spain with a concrete fist for the best part of four decades (see box, page 46).

Hurry through Ferrol's outskirts and modern expansions, some of the more depressing urban landscapes in modern Spain. In some of the poorer, high-density areas, the council inexcusably hasn't even bothered to give the streets proper names; just letters. Nevertheless, the city centre conserves a certain maritime charm, and the council is making big efforts to spruce the place up to encourage a bit of tourism to this unfashionable place.

Waterfront
Although the waterfront is mostly taken up by naval buildings and dockyards, it's well worth strolling along: from the **Paseo de la Marina** at the western tip of the old town, you can get a good idea of just how large Ferrol's excellent natural

harbour (the Ría do Ferrol) is. Near here is one of the twin forts defending the port. Another, **Castillo de San Felipe** ⓘ *daily 1100-1830, free,* is worth visiting further around the bay if you have your own transport. Most of Ferrol's character is in the five or six parallel streets back from here. The elegant balconied buildings tell of days of prosperity, as do the several *indiano* buildings. The whitewashed neoclassical church and post office show some of these influences; nearby is the busy modern market. Franco was born on Rúa María, four streets back from the shore at No 136 (although the street was called Frutos Saavedra when he was a nipper).

From the waterfront, hour-long cruises run hourly from July to September, costing €7, T620 926 958 for details. You could also take a boat across the bay to **Mugardos** (€3 each way) for a seafoody lunch.

Tourist information

There are several tourist offices around town. They have a number of themed leaflets in Spanish on various aspects of the city that are also downloadable from www.ferrol.es (navigate to Turismo, then Guías de Turismo, and you'll find English-language downloads).

Marina tourist office
Paseo da Marina s/n. Mon-Sat 1000-1400, 1600-2000, Sun 1000-1400.

Regional tourist office
Rúa Magdalena 12, T981 337 131. Mon-Sat 1000-1400, 1600-1900 (1700-2000 summer), Sun 1000-1400.

Where to stay

Ferrol has several modern business hotels and lots of low-budget options, not all of them good.

€€€ Parador de Ferrol
Rúa Almirante Fernández Martín s/n, T981 356 720, www.parador.es.

Situated in a good spot, at the end of the old town near the water, this parador has comfortable rooms, many with views, although these cost a little more.

€ Hostal da Madalena
Rúa Magdalena 98, T981 355 615, www.hostalmadalena.com.
Clean and cheap and far better than some of the seedier options around Ferrol. Smart renovated rooms and free Wi-Fi make this a reliable budget choice.

Restaurants

Across the bay, Mugardos has some good and traditionally Galician seafood places.

€€ Casa Rivera
Rúa Galiano 57, T981 350 759.
This well-priced restaurant has excellent seafood and land-based dishes, with cheering stews and tasty octopus.

Bars and clubs

Ferrol has a lively bar scene, mostly centred in the old town.

Transport

The **FEVE** station, **RENFE** station and bus station are close together near Praza de España a short way north of the old centre.

Bus
There are very frequent services to **A Coruña**. **Santiago**, **Pontevedra**, **Vigo**, **Betanzos** and the north coast are also regularly serviced by bus.

Ferry
A launch service zips across the *ría* to **Mugardos** from Paseo de la Marina. Mugardos is a pretty little fishing town; you might want to stay for lunch and try the famed local recipe for octopus.

Train
4 **FEVE** trains a day head eastwards towards **Oviedo**; 2 of them only make it to **Ribadeo**. There's 4-5 daily trains between Ferrol and **A Coruña** (1¼ hrs).

Pontedeume and the Caaveiro Valley
a solitary monastery surrounded by Atlantic forest

South of Ferrol, the river mouth town of Pontedeume is a prettier and more relaxed place to hang out despite the almost constant line of traffic through town. Its main features are its long bridge across the Eume and an impressive 14th-century tower. Both were originally built by the Andrade family, local lairds, *bon viveurs* and boar hunters (see page 60). A weathered stone boar faces across the bridge.

"The valley of Caaveiro", wrote Richard Ford in the mid-19th century, "is one of the most secluded in Spain". Not much has changed. The valley, part of the Fragas do Eume natural park, is an important zone of Atlantic forest and refuge of much wildlife; there are many otters (mostly further up, above the hydroelectric station), boar, ermine and birds. Fishing has been suspended on the river to allow the salmon and trout levels to restabilize.

Monasterio de San Xoán de Caaveiro
Visits at 1100, 1200, 1300, 1530, 1630 weekends only in winter, daily in summer, free.

At the end of the valley road, some 13 km east of Pontedeume, is this atmospheric ruined monastery. It was founded by the boy-bishop San Rosendo in the 10th century. The remaining Romanesque walls look over the river; it's a lovely setting.

Nearby, a rapid watercourse feeds the Eume with yet more water. From the monastery, you may want to strike off for a walk: the **GR50 long-distance path** crosses the bridge at the monastery. The whole walk is recommended; it stretches from Betanzos to Cabo Ortegal at the top of Galicia, and can be done comfortably in four days, or strenuously in two. A shorter walk takes you past the monastery on the yellow-marked PR path back downstream for 3 km; you can then cross via a bridge and return up the road to your car.

The road's not designed to handle much traffic, so at busy periods, like summer weekends, you may have to leave your car at the visitors centre and travel to the monastery in a minibus.

ON THE ROAD
Generalísimo Franco

"A less straightforward man I never met" John Whitaker, American journalist. Francisco Franco y Bahamonde looms over 20th-century Spanish history like the concrete monoliths he was so fond of building and, like them, his shadow is long. Born in 1892 in the Galician naval port of Ferrol, this son of a naval administrator wanted to join the navy but was forced to choose the army due to lack of places at the academy. Sent to the war in Morocco at the age of 20, he excelled, showing remarkable military ability and bravery. As commander of the new Foreign Legion, he was largely responsible for the victory achieved there in 1925; this success saw him made Spain's youngest ever general at the age of 33.

The authoritarian Franco was just the man the government needed to put down the rebellion of the Asturian miners in 1934; this he achieved brutally. Having been sent to a command in the Canaries, out of harm's way as the government thought, he agreed to join the conspiracy against the Republic fairly late. Once the rising was underway, he took command of the army in Morocco, which was transported across to the Spanish mainland with German assistance, a crucial intervention in the context of the war.

Franco's advance was successful and rapid – he soon manoeuvred his way into the Nationalist leadership, reluctantly being given supreme power by his fellow generals. He assumed the title of *Caudillo*, or 'head' and installed himself in Burgos.

Throughout the war, he was known for his ruthlessness, never more so than when the German Condor Legion razed Gernika from the air on market day, killing numerous civilians. After the Nationalist victory, the Generalísimo

There are other access roads to the natural park; one crosses it north to south running between the towns of A Capela and Monfero.

Listings Pontedeume and the Caaveiro Valley

Tourist information

Pontedume Tourist Office
In the tower.
Staff advise on things to see in the area, of which there are several.

Information centre
A short way into the valley (coming from the north, cross the bridge in Pontedeume, bear left, then take the 1st left turn; follow this road for a while, then bear left again; it's signposted Caaveiro), T981 432 528. Daily 0900-1400, 1600-1900 (2000 summer).
This office has maps of walks.

Where to stay

There are several lodging options in Pontedeume and several *casas rurales* in the area.

showed no signs of giving up power, although in 1949 he declared himself as a regent pending the choice of a king. He ensured that there was to be no leniency for those who had supported the former Republic and a cruel purge followed. Franco wasn't exactly relaxed and charismatic; after meeting him in 1940 to discuss possible Spanish involvement in the Second World War, Adolf Hitler said he "would rather have three or four teeth out" than meet him again.

After the war Franco's dictatorship was shunned by the western democracies until Cold War realpolitik made the USA adopt him as an ally, betraying the governments-in-exile they had continued to recognize. A massive aid package in exchange for military bases gave Franco the cash required to begin modernizing a country that had been crippled by the Civil War, but for much of his rule parts of Spain remained undeveloped. Eventually the Franco government was recognized by other countries, and Spain was accepted into the UN, but remained politically and culturally stagnant. Separatism was not countenanced; Franco banned Euskara and even Galego, the tongue of his native Galicia. He never forgot an enemy; the regions that had struggled to uphold democracy were left to rot while he conferred favours on the Nationalist heartlands of Castilla and Navarra. The ageing dictator appointed Juan Carlos, grandson of the former king, as his designated successor in 1969.

Franco died in 1975: "*Españoles*" – the Spanish people were solemnly informed – "*Franco ha muerto*". The man described as "a sphinx without a secret" was no more: those who mourned the passing of this plump, shy, suspicious, authoritarian general were comparatively few, but Francoism is still alive within the Spanish political right, and memorial services on the anniversaries of his death are still held.

€€ Casa do Castelo de Andrade
Castelo de Andrade s/n, T981 433 839, www.castelo andrade.com.
About 8 km southeast of Pontedeume, this standout rural hotel comprises 3 old farm buildings in an isolated spot surrounded by meadows and woodland. They've been beautifully converted and the blend of the historic stone with modern design features makes it a wonderfully romantic place to stay for a couple of days. Recommended.

€€ Casa Graña da Acea
Acea, near Monfero, T981 788 282, www.casaturismoruralcoruna.com.
Just 2 km from the town of Monfero (labelled Rebordelo on some maps), near the natural park, this wonderful converted old stone house makes a great rural retreat. Rooms are all different but decorated with rustic style; the courteous sisters who run it put on good home-cooked dinners.

€€ Hotel Eumesa
Av de A Coruña s/n, T981 430 925, www.hoteleumesa.es.
In the centre of Pontedeume, this simple and friendly hotel has decent rooms, many overlooking the river mouth. There's some traffic noise. Breakfast included.

€ Allegue
Rúa Chafaris 1, T981 430 035,
www.hostalallegue.com.
A little place with clean and comfortable
rooms with simple bathrooms and an
attractive patio.

Bus and train
The train service between **Ferrol** and
A Coruña calls at Pontedeume, as do
buses on the same route.

A Coruña &
the Costa da Morte

One of Spain's most enjoyable cities to visit, A Coruña is
spectacularly situated and has a superb atmosphere. It's
a place where, at least when it's not raining, everyone
seems to stay outdoors enjoying the privileged natural
setting. Coruña has a bit of everything; a harbour, a
good beach, top seafood, great nightlife, Romanesque
architecture, entertaining museums, quiet corners and
a have-a-go football team. It's an excellent town for
the tourist but also still an important working port and
commercial centre.

The rugged coast west of A Coruña is named the 'coast
of death', and has an interesting and dark history of
marine disasters, wreckers and 'five and twenty ponies
trotting through the dark' smuggling. There are some
excellent beaches and some fairly authentic towns,
which get on with their fishing and farming as the
majority of tourists zip straight down to Finisterre.

★One of the best ways to take in A Coruña's sights is a walk starting in the old town by the port and continuing anticlockwise around the headland. It's a long stroll, but you can hop on the tram that circles the route about every half-hour (weekends only in winter).

Essential A Coruña

Finding your feet

Most of A Coruña can be easily explored on foot. The coastal *paseo* around the headland is a long one, but a tourist tram covers the route half-hourly; a beautiful ride. The bus and train stations are a 20- to 30-minute walk south from the centre of town. City bus No 1 runs from the main road between the bus and train stations into town.

Best places to eat

Domus, page 57
Pablo Gallego, page 57
Taberna da Penela, page 58

When to go

Two days will let you appreciate most of the sights, but add an extra day for lounging on the beach.

Tip...

A Coruña has a superb tapas scene, with *pulpo* (octopus) the excellent local speciality. It's usually served boiled, simply garnished with *pimentón* (similar to paprika), olive oil and salt, and accompanied by *cachelos* (boiled spuds). If you don't mind the slimy texture, it's superb.

Avenida de la Marina and around

The Avenida de la Marina is a good place to start. It's a very elegant boulevard lined with attractive old houses with trademark *galerías* or miradors, windowed balconies that look out over the water. Off here is the **Praza María Pita**, named after the city's heroine. The arcaded square is centred on a statue of María herself, defiantly brandishing a spear with a couple of Drake's mercenaries dead at her feet. She is commemorated with an eternal flame and faces the **Ayuntamiento**, a Galician *modernista* building.

A few block north of Avenida de la Marina is the modern **Museo de Bellas Artes** ⓘ *Av Zalaeta s/n, Tue-Fri 1000-2000, Sat 1000-1400, 1630-2000, Sun 1000-1400, €2.40,* an excellent space that incorporates part of a former monastery and has a reasonable collection of European art, including some Goya sketches and some works by Rubens, as well as lesser-known but worthwhile Galician artists. Another place with good temporary art exhibitions is the striking **Centro Sociocultural Nova Caixa Galicia** ⓘ *Cantón Grande 21, T981 185 060, www.fundacioncaixagalicia. org, Mon-Sat 0900-2100.*

Ciudad Vieja East from the Praza María Pita is a very attractive network of old town streets, Ciudad Vieja, a quiet place with some fine houses, squares and churches. The church of

BACKGROUND

A Coruña

Such a fine natural harbour as Coruña's was pounced upon early; it was used by the Celts and Phoenicians before becoming an important Roman port, Ardobicum Coronium. It was said that the foundations were laid by Hercules himself. The city remained (and remains) a significant port; it was the westernmost member of the **Hermandad de las Marismas**, a trading league formed in 1296 along Hanseatic lines.

Coruña's northward orientation is historically linked with Britain, whose sailors referred to it as 'the Groyne'. British pilgrims used to disembark here en route to the tomb of Saint James. This *Camino Inglés* was the easiest of the Pilgrim Routes to Santiago, at least when the Bay of Biscay was in clement mood.

In 1386 John of Gaunt, son of Edward III, decided to avenge the murder of his father-in-law, Pedro I, and landed here with an army. After a farcical progress through Galicia, a peace was finally brokered whereby John's daughter would marry the heir to the Castilian throne. The Castilian king compensated him for the expenses occurred in the invasion and he went home, honour satisfied.

When John's great-granddaughter, the Catholic Monarch Isabel, died, Philip the Fair of Flanders landed here in 1506 to meet with Fernando and claim the Castilian throne. His grandson Philip II had plenty to do with Coruña too; while still a prince, he embarked from here to England, where he married Mary at Winchester. Some 34 years later he assembled his Armada, whose 130 ships put out from the harbour here with 30,000 men. In 1507 Francis Drake had also sailed here and set fire to the town but was thwarted by the town's heroine María Pita, who saved Coruña by seizing the British standard and rallying the townsfolk to repel the buccaneers.

In 1809 a dispirited and undisciplined British army were relentlessly pursued by the Napoleonic forces of Marshal Soult. Having abandoned all their baggage and gold, the army made for Coruña where a fleet was stationed, but Soult was hard on their heels. To save as many men as possible, the Scottish general, Sir John Moore, faced the French with a small force while 15,000 troops embarked on to the ships. Moore was killed and the force defeated, but the majority of the army got away thanks to the sacrifice.

Compared with other Spanish cities, Coruña thrived in the 19th and 20th centuries; it seems its close ties to northern Europe and its flourishing port saved it from stagnation.

Santa María del Campo is a charming Romanesque building dating from the late 13th century. Its wide nave and narrow aisles make for an intriguing interior space, with a crooked, off-centre alignment and solid barrel vaulting. The 13th-century portal is a good work, as is the later rose window. In the eaves, a curious carved pattern looks like dripping wax. The side portal also features elegant

Romanesque stonework. Alongside, there's a small **museum** ⓘ *Tue-Fri 1000-1300, 1700-1900, Sat 1000-1300, free,* of religious art.

A Coruña

Where to stay 🛏
Carbonara **1**
Centro Gallego **2**
Hesperia Finisterre **4**
Hospedaje Os
  Potes **3**
Hostal Mara **6**
Hostal Palas **5**
La Provinciana **7**
Meliá María Pita **8**
Riazor **9**
Santa Catalina **11**

Restaurants 🍴
Albeiro **2**
Alcume **3**
A Mundiña **5**
A Taberna de Cunqueiro **8**
Café Tortoni **4**

N
100 metres
100 yards

Jardín de San Carlos *"Not a drum was heard, nor a funeral note, as his corse to the ramparts we hurried"*, Charles Wolfe. The small and evocative Jardín de San Carlos is the final resting place of General Sir John Moore, the Scot who turned "like a lion

ON THE ROAD

Zara

A major Galician success story, the fashion retailer Zara began in 1963 in the bedroom of founders Amancio Ortega and his late ex-wife Rosalía Mera, making white labcoats. They were successful enough to be able to open the first Zara shop in central A Coruña in 1975, and quickly grew through Spain, expanding into Portugal in 1988. The group now has some 6000 stores in 85 countries and Ortega is Spain's wealthiest person.

Zara's stablemates in the Inditex group include Bershka and Pull & Bear, aimed at a younger market, Massimo Dutti, slightly more upmarket, and the cutting-edge Stradivarius, as well as other labels. The group still produces a majority of its products in Spain, and has attracted attention for Ortega's preference for anonymity, reluctance to spend much on advertising and progressive management techniques.

at bay" to engage the superior French forces of Marshal Soult to give his dispirited army time to embark on the waiting ships. He was killed by a cannonball and hurriedly buried "by the struggling moonbeam's misty light". The soldier's grave was later marked with a granite monument; in Spain, the Peninsular War is named the War of Independence, and British involvement fondly remembered, although the redcoats' behaviour and discipline was frequently atrocious. Poems by Charles Wolfe and Rosalía de Castro commemorate Moore, and fresh flowers often appear on the grave.

The marina and around Descending from here to the marina, the fort that juts into the bay was built by Felipe II and now houses the **Museo Histórico Arqueológico** ① *Sep-Jun Tue-Sat 1000-1930, Sun 1000-1430, Jul and Aug Tue-Sat 1000-2100, Sun 1000-1500, €2, free Sat*, the highlight of which is a number of pieces of Celtic jewellery including distinctive torcs and the famous 'helmet of Leiro'.

East of here, the massive glass **cuboids** of the port authority's control tower cut an impressive figure. From here, you might want to get the tram around to the Torre de Hércules, as it's a 20-minute walk with little of interest (apart from the great waterfront views).

The **Torre de Hércules** ① *Oct-May 1000-1800, Jun-Sep 1000-2100, €3*, stands very proud at the northern tip of Coruña's peninsula. It was originally built in the second century AD by the Romans, and claims to be the oldest lighthouse still operational. Its current exterior dates from an 18th-century reformation and, in truth, there's not much Roman left of it, apart from a central core and some foundations, visible in a low-ceilinged space before you ascend. It's worth climbing the 234 steps to the top, where there's a good view of A Coruña and the coast.

Not far beyond the lighthouse is the **aquarium** ① *daily 1000-2100, last entry an hour before, €10 (€12 for combined ticket to here, Casa de Ciencias and Domus)*. There are good displays (no English) on lots of aspects of sea life, an outdoor seal pool, an intriguing tank with growing fish embryos, and a curious underground observation area decked out to look like Nemo's office in the Nautilus.

The ark-like **Domus** ① *daily 1000-2000, €2 (€4 including IMAX projection; combined ticket with aquarium and Casa de las Ciencias €12)*, looks like the hull of a boat and has become something of a city emblem since famed Japanese architect Arata Isozaki created it. It's an entertaining modern museum of humankind, dealing in all aspects of how we function physically and mentally. There are loads of interactive exhibits, giving plenty of fun for young and old. There's also a café.

Beyond the old town The curve of the city's excellent beach sweeps around the bay. It's a top stretch of sand, slightly marred by poor waterfront architecture. Although there's plenty of space, in summer it can be packed out. At its far end is the **Estadio de Riazor**. The city's football team, Deportivo La Coruña, small by European standards, have achieved many notable successes.

In the Santa Margarita park, the **Casa de las Ciencias** ① *daily 1000-2000, €2, planetarium €2 (combined ticket with aquarium and Domus €12)*, has good displays on biology and mechanics as well as a planetarium, which can be dogged by lengthy queues.

Listings A Coruña *map p52*

Tourist information

A Coruña has several tourist offices. The most useful are listed below.

Municipal office
On the main square, Plaza María Pita 6, T981 923 093, www.turismocoruna.com. Mon-Fri 0900-2030, Sat 1000-1400, 1600-2000, Sun 1000-1500.

Regional office
On the marina, not far from the municipal office, T981 221 822, oficina. turismo.coruna@xunta.es. Mon-Fri 1000-1400, 1600-1900, Sat 1100-1400, 1700-1900, Sun 1100-1400.

Where to stay

A Coruña has a large number of good-quality budget accommodation options, concentrated in the tapas zone a couple of streets back from Av de la Marina. All choices are notably cheaper outside Jul and Aug. Expect street noise in central-zone hotels at weekends.

€€€ Hotel Hesperia Finisterre
Paseo del Parrote 2, T981 205 400, www.hesperia-hoteles.com.
Superbly located on the headland, this is the nicest place to stay in A Coruña. Rooms are smallish but bright, furnished with style, and many have superb views over the harbour and sea. There are all the facilities you could ask for, and an excellent restaurant. Recommended.

€€€ Hotel Riazor
Av de Pedro Barrié de la Maza 29, T981 253 400, www.riazorhotel.com.
This is a big but pleasant beachfront hotel near the stadium. Some rooms have really great views – make sure you specify that you want one when reserving. It's a lot cheaper outside high summer.

€€€ Meliá María Pita

Av Pedro Barrié de la Maza 1,
T981 205 000, www.melia.com.
Cavernously large, this imposing
business hotel has an excellent location
overlooking the city beach. Rooms that
actually have water views cost a little
more, but are worth it, as other views are
rather uninspiring. Service is courteous,
but extras are expensive. Good off-
season rates (€€).

€€ Carbonara

Rúa Nueva 16, T981 225 251,
www.hostalcarbonara.com.
One of the better choices, this is a very
good central spot with super-friendly
management and decent rooms with
bathrooms in a typically attractive
Coruña house. It's in the heart of the
tapas zone.

€€ Centro Gallego

C Estrella 2, T981 222 236, www.
pensioncentrogallego.com.
This is a very good option above a
friendly café, with no-frills but excellent-
value rooms with decent bathrooms.
It's a remarkably good deal considering
its proximity to water, tourist office, bars
and octopus taverns. Off season, it's
one of the cheapest places in town.

€€ Hotel Santa Catalina

C Fernando Arenas Quintela 1, T981 226
704, www.hotelstacatalina.es.
Right in the heart of Coruña with top
tapas a couple of steps from the door,
this recently remodelled choice has
upgraded from *hostal* to hotel status
but still offers a very reasonable rate
for comfortable accommodation.

€€ La Provinciana

Rúa Nueva 7, T981 220 400,
www.laprovinciana.net.

An excellent spot to stay off season, as
the rooms are good and drop to a very
low price. The rooms are heated and
there's parking available; it's a good deal.
Although not exactly charismatic, it's run
with old-fashioned courtesy.

€ Hospedaje Os Potes

C Zapatería 15, T981 205 219.
This simple but comfortable budget
option is beautifully located in a narrow
street in the heart of the old part of
Coruña, near the delightfully wobbly
Plaza Azcárraga.

€ Hostal Mara

C Galera 49, T981 221 802,
www.hostalmara.com.
In tapas bar heartland, this is a reliable
option with good, clean en suite doubles
at the quiet end of the street. They're
sound people running it, and there's a
decent cheap restaurant. Good value
off-season. Parking available.

€ Hostal Palas

C Marqués de Amboage 21, T981 247 400,
www.pensionpalas.com.
This is a good option if you arrive late
or are leaving early; it's right next to the
bus station and just across the overpass
from the train station. It's run by cheerful
old folk and is modern and clean as a
whistle. They're used to people coming
and going at odd hours.

Restaurants

A Coruña has a superb tapas scene,
with *pulpo* (octopus) the excellent local
speciality. It's usually served boiled,
simply garnished with paprika, olive oil
and salt, and accompanied by *cachelos*
(boiled spuds). If you don't mind the
slimy texture, it's superb.

From the Plaza de María Pita, C Franja
and its continuations Galera, and

(especially recommended) Estrella, form the heart of the eating zone. They are wall-to-wall *tascas*, simple spots with small tables and few frills dealing out delicious *raciones*; most locals eat in this way, hence, there are comparatively few traditional restaurants. There's little purpose to a lengthy list of recommendations; just wend your way along that route and pick a place you like. They're nearly all good: the more locals inside, the better.

€€€ A Mundiña
C Estrella 10, T881 899 327, www.amunidna.com.
With warm and stylish decoration, this place stands out on the popular C Estrella strip. Places around here live and die by the quality of their seafood, and this makes the grade with comfort. Prices are a little higher than you might pay elsewhere, but they go the extra mile on things like service, wine list, and so on.

€€€ Domus
C Novoa Santos 15, T981 201 136, www.casapardo-domus.com.
The people that ran one of Coruña's best-regarded fish restaurants now run the restaurant in the Domus museum. Great views, good service and excellent food make a winning combination. Recommended. Coruña's finest restaurant treats its fish just right and is far from overpriced. It also does delicious partridge in season and good salads too. The seafood croquettes are justly famed. The decor is modern and stylish. Recommended.

€€€ El Manjar
C Alfredo Vicenti 29, T981 142 552.
A cosy restaurant with excellent old-time decor near the Riazor Stadium. They do

a great *zarzuela de pescado* (fish stew) and succulent *chipirones*. Their tortilla is famous across Galicia. Don't expect what you want to be available; just ask for whatever's good that day; it's that sort of place.

€€€ Pablo Gallego
C Capitán Trancoso 4, T981 208 888, www.pablogallego.com.
In a new location just around the corner from the picturesque central square, this intimate, romantic restaurant deals out good-quality seafood with a confident modern slant. Service is formal but friendly and there's a long wine list. Recommended.

€€ A Taberna de Cunqueiro
C Estrella 22, T981 212 629.
With warm, enticing decor and helpful service, this popular tapas bar attracts a loyal following. They'll serve you a free snack with your glass of decent wine. Locals get rid of their pesky copper coins by sticking them in cracks in the stone wall.

€€ Albeiro
C de la Franja, T981 224 592.
Simply decorated, this old-fashioned restaurant is a reliable choice for fruits of the sea just off the plaza. They do a good mixed grill of fish, as well as tasty *cigalas* and other seafood.

€€ O Bo
C Menéndez Pelayo 18, T981 927 237.
A traditional type of place, this sticks to what the Galicians know best; all the recipes have been handed down for generations. The *cocido gallego* is a guaranteed winter warmer, while the *pulpo* is delicious and other typical dishes reliable.

€€ Taberna da Penela
Plaza María Pita 9, T981 209 200, www.lapenela.com.
Buzzing with chatter and conviviality, this lively spot with a terrace on the main square is an excellent place to eat. The octopus is superb and backed up by tasty fish and meat dishes as well as swift service. There's a quieter, more formal restaurant, **La Penela**, with similar prices and dishes, just around the square at no 12.

€ Alcume
C Galera 44, T981 210 174.
A wooden-clad BBQ restaurant on the main tapas strip, this Argentine-style eatery has a cosy front terrace and tempting smells of grilled meats. No-frills options like chorizo *criollo* or *costilla* (ribs) are exceedingly tasty and priced low.

€ El Serrano
C Galera 21, T981 220 353.
If all that seafood is starting to make you feel a bit jaded, stop off here for excellent hams and cheeses, including the great Basque Idiazábal. They do several *tablas* (mixed boards) that are great for sharing.

€ Mesón do Pulpo
C de la Franja 9, T981 202 444.
The name says it all; on the street of octopus, this place does some of the best; just follow the locals. There are several choices of our 8-legged friend, and also a good selection of other seafood.

Cafés

Café Tortoni
Cantón Grande 21, T981 185 060.
This posh, modern open-plan space occupies part of the ground floor of the Fundación Caixa Galicia building. It's a popular spot for tasty, good-value breakfasts and also has several internet terminals. Their coffee is great.

Bars and clubs

After tapas time is over, folk tend to move on to 1 of 2 areas. A smarter scene goes on in the streets around Praza España and the Museo de Bellas Artes. A more alternative crowd hangs out in the bars and clubs around C del Sol, C Barrera and C Juan Canalejo de Corralón between the tapas zone and the beach. It's dead on weekdays, but at weekends it's as lively as anywhere in Northern Spain. Wander around and take your pick.

Portofino
C Estrella 15, www.restaurante portofino.es, T981 902 110.
The indoor-outdoor vibe of this place takes in coffee, tapas, set menus for lunch and dinner, wines, and more, but it really gets going around midnight with beers and mixed drinks: the horseshoe bar defends a veritable citadel of spirits.

Entertainment

Centro Rosales, *Rosales, T981 128 092, www.yelmocineplex.es*. A very big cinema complex in a shopping centre.
Palacio de la Opera, *T981 140 404, www.palaciodelaopera.com*. As well as being an opera venue, this is the home ground of the Galician symphony orchestra.

Festivals

Aug Coruña's main festival is in honour of **María Pita** and lasts the whole month, with all sorts of cultural events and a mock naval battle. The main week, **Semana Grande**, is in the middle of Aug.

Shopping

C del Real, *1 street back from Av de la Marina*, is the handiest shopping street.

What to do

Diving
Centro de Buceo Nauga, *Manuel Azaña 41, T981 129 811, www.nauga.es*. Offer diving courses and equipment rental.

Transport

Air
A Coruña Airport (LCG) lies to the south of the city. There are international flights to **Lisbon** and **London** Heathrow, as well as national ones to **Madrid**, **Barcelona**, and **Sevilla**.

Buses run regularly from Puerta Real to the airport (€1.40). There's also a daily bus (leaving at 1030, T981 257 082) from the **Hotel Atlántico**, Jardines Méndez Núñez, to the international airport at **Santiago**. A taxi to the centre is €20-25.

Bicycle hire
There's a municipal bike rental shed on Paseo de la Dársena by the leisure harbour. Open 0900-2100 summer; 0900-1400, 1600-2100 winter. A 2-hr rental is €6; a whole day is €21. **Eco-Lógica**, C Cantábrico 2, T981 904 040, are open daily and rent cheap fold-up bikes, better 'slim' bikes and Segways

Bus
The bus station is to the south of town, on C de Caballeros. Frequent buses (No 1) connect it with the city centre. Within Galicia, **Ourense** is served 8 times daily, **Lugo** 11 times, **Santiago** hourly (via motorway 45 mins, via road 1 hr 20 mins), **Pontevedra** and **Vigo** 9 times, **Betanzos** 6 times, and **Ferrol** hourly. 5 buses daily go down the **Costa da Morte** to **Camariñas**.

Long-distance destinations include **Gijón/Oviedo** (4 a day, 5-6 hrs), **Bilbao** (2 daily, 11 hrs) via **Santander** and **Madrid** (6-7 daily, 7 hrs).

Train
The train station is just across the main road, and up the hill from the bus station. **Santiago** (45 mins) and **Vigo** (2 hrs) are serviced roughly hourly. There are also trains to **Lugo** (2 daily, 1 hr 30 mins), **Ourense** (4 daily, 2 hrs 15 mins), **Madrid** (2 daily, 8 hrs), and **Barcelona** (1-2 daily, 14½ hrs).

Around A Coruña
traditional Galician town with well-preserved medieval churches

Betanzos
The town of Betanzos makes a good day trip from A Coruña. The site of a Celtic settlement, and a significant Roman port, it's an attractive, if slightly faded place that was dealt a bitter blow in the 17th and 18th centuries when the port silted up and Betanzos gradually became an inland town, although it's still a junction of the two pretty rivers that are to blame for the fiasco. In summer you can take a boat trip on them. Betanzos's main attraction is its steep streets lined with trademark Galician housing. There are a couple of nice plazas and four churches, of which the highlight is **Iglesia de San Francisco**. In the **Praza Constitución** there's a small museum devoted to modern prints. Buses stop on the road across the river from the old town.

Iglesia de San Francisco This monastery church, built in the 14th century, is the highlight of Betanzos. It was paid for by the count Fernán de Andrade, lord over most of this region, and dubbed 'O Bóo', or the good; it's not clear by whom, probably himself. He had the church built with his own soul in mind: he intended to rest in peace in it, but wasn't prepared to compromise. His earthly love was boarhunting, and the number of carved boars both outside and in the church is noteworthy. The top attraction, however, is his tomb (although he's not actually in it). It's carved with excellent hunting scenes, all dogs, horns, and tally-hos, and is mounted on the back of a large stone boar and a rather brainless-looking bear. There are many other tombs of lords and ladies, as well as some representations of saints. The apse is big and light and holds a simple sculpture of Saint Francis and the Crucifixion behind the altar. The vaulting is elaborate, but the pigs still pull focus.

Iglesia de Santa María del Azogue Dating from the 14th century, this church has a pleasant, spacious interior with some slightly skewed columns with good carved capitals. The *retablo* is dark and is centred on an icon of the Virgin. The façade features the elders of the Apocalypse around a scene of the Adoration on the tympanum. Strange animals adorn the capitals.

Iglesia de Santiago ⓘ *1000-1400, 1700-2100, €1.* This church dates from the 15th century and has a very fine carved portal of Santiago Matamoros and the Pantocrator. The capitals on either side of the door are carved with frightening beasts. The interior is simple, with a triple nave. There are six buses a day between Betanzos and Coruña, and a couple to Santiago.

Listings Around A Coruña

Tourist information

Betanzos Tourist Office
Behind the church on the plaza on the main road through town.

Where to stay

Betanzos

€€ Hotel Garelos
C Alfonso IX 8, T981 775 922, www.hotelgarelos.com.
Betanzos doesn't have a huge variety of accommodation, but this is a good central option, with quiet, spacious rooms, handsome decor and public spaces.

Camping

El Raso
T981 460 676.
A campsite near Betanzos by the beach of the same name. It's open year-round and there's an on-site café.

Restaurants

Betanzos
The bars with outdoor seats on the big Plaza Mayor do decent tapas.

€€ Os Arcos
C Argentina 6, T981 772 259.
A friendly local restaurant. They also do decent budget accommodation.

enchanting untamed coastline with a dark history

★This stretch of coast gets its name from the many ships that have been wrecked along its treacherous rocky shoreline. It can be wild, windy and desolate at times but the lack of development and beautiful coves will appeal to those looking to avoid the busier resorts further south.

Malpica

The first stop of interest along from A Coruña is Malpica, a lively, unadulterated fishing town ruled by a pack of large and brazen Atlantic seagulls. There's an offshore nesting sanctuary for less forceful seabirds on the **Islas Sisargas** opposite. You can get out to the islands by chartering a boat for about €20 per person (minimum €100), T652 943 960. Malpica also has a good beach, which can get pretty good surf.

Corme

There are some good wild beaches west of here. The town of Corme is reached via a side road, and sits on a nice bay used to cultivate shellfish. The port is backed by narrow streets tightly packed with the houses of fishing families. Bypass the town beach and head for **Praia Ermida**, 1 km or so further around the bay. The town doesn't give too much away; it was known as a nest of anti-Franco guerrilla activity during the Civil War, and anybody prying into the coming and going of boats in the middle of the night these days might end up sleeping with the shellfish. Over 2600 kg of cocaine were captured in one of the higher-profile police raids in 2006. A more traditional maritime harvest is the *percebe*, or goose-necked barnacle; the *perceberos* who collect them have a perilous job, but it's a much-appreciated Galician speciality.

Ponteceso and around

Ponteceso has a bridge of medieval origins that crosses the marshy river. If it's beaches you want, stop at **Laxe**, which has a top strand of white sand, and an even better one to the west; peaceful **Praia Traba**. The town itself isn't great.

Camariñas

The coast continues to be impressive; Camariñas, the next worthwhile place from Ponteceso, makes a good place to stop. It's famous throughout Spain for its lace; if that's not your thing, it also enjoys a privileged location, on a pretty inlet stocked with pines and eucalypts. It looks across the *ría* to Muxía on the other side. The port is small but serious, with some biggish boats heading far out to sea. There's a summer-only **tourist office** on the *ría*-side *paseo*.

The **Museo do Encaixe** ① *T981 736 340, mid-Jun to Aug Tue-Sat 1100-1400, 1700-2000, Sun 1100-1400, 1700-1900, Sep closed, Oct to mid-Jun Thu-Sat 1100-1400, 1600-1900, Sun 1100-1400, 1600-1800, otherwise call first, €2*, details the history and practice of lacemaking; they make it bobbin-style here. It is famous throughout

ON THE ROAD
Shipwrecks and smugglers

The indentations and rocks that abound on Galicia's coastline provide some spectacular scenery but also have a darker side. It is a sobering fact that in the last century some 140 ships have gone down with the loss of over 500 lives. The scandalously mismanaged *Prestige* oil disaster in 2002 is just one of a long series of shipping incidents on this coast.

Local legend attributes many of these wrecks to the activities of *raqueiros* (wreckers), who lured ships onto the rocks by attaching lights to the horns of cattle. More likely though, it is the combination of sea-surges and savage rocks that make this coast so hazardous.

The natural features of the coast that make it so dangerous for shipping have made it a haven for smugglers down the years. Not long ago, Galicia's smugglers moved away from more traditional products towards drugs. A large proportion of Europe's cocaine arrived through Galicia, usually being left well offshore by a smugglers' ship, then picked up by one of the coast's fishing fleet. Recently, heavy police activity has seen much of this trade move to other locations.

Spain, and can be bought at several outlets in the village; on a nice day you may even see some elderly lacemakers at work in the sun outside their houses.

The best thing to do in Camariñas is explore the **headland** to the north. There's a series of dirt roads that are just about driveable, but it's nicer on foot with the smell of pine in your nose. **Cabo Vilán** is about an hour's walk, a dramatic spot with a big lighthouse building and high, modern windmills, which work pretty hard here. Further east, there are a small **beaches** and an English cemetery, with the graves of some of the dead of a British navy vessel wrecked on the coast in 1890, at a cost of 170 lives.

Muxía

The counterpart of Camariñas on the other side of the *ría*, Muxía is a tightly packed fishing town that makes up for in authenticity what it lacks in postcardy charm. It's worth visiting, though, to see the **Santuario de Nuestra Señora de la Barca** on a headland just past the town. With the waves beating the rocks to a pulp around the chapel, it's a hugely atmospheric place; it's not hard to see why fisherfolk who brave the stormy seas have a healthy religious and superstitious streak around here. The spot was originally venerated to commemorate an impressive navigational feat in the early first century AD; the Virgin Mary sailed from Palestine to this very spot in a stone boat. If you don't believe it, take a look inside the church: various fragments of the vessel are set around the sloping interior. Now, fishermen pray for the safety of their own boats, often leaving small models as ex-voto offerings.

On the first Sunday after 8 September, there's an important *romería* to the sanctuary in Muxía; part of the ritual is a claustrophobic crawl under a huge rock. It's one of the most atmospheric and meaningful of Galicia's fiestas.

Corcubión and Cée

At the foot of the Finisterre peninsula, the fishing ports of Corcubión and Cée have grown into each other, stretching around the bay. It's a fairly serious fishing spot, and Corcubión is the epitome of a picturesque Galician fishing town, with plenty of hotels and restaurants. Cée has a small ship-wrecking industry, a fairly tough business, but nothing compared to what confronts you a little further around the bay; a giant alloys plant that manages to effectively recreate Hell on the Galician coast. Pity the workers.

Listings Costa da Morte

Where to stay

Malpica

€€ Hostal JB
C Playa 3, T981 721 906,
www.hostaljbmalpica.com.
This is a good bet, with appealing rooms overlooking the beach. Great value and cordially run.

€€ Hotel Fonte do Fraile
Playa de Canido s/n, T981 720 732,
www.hotelfontedofraile.com.
Right on the beach, this 3-star hotel is the most luxurious option hereabouts. Its rooms are all distinctly and beautifully decorated, airy and spacious. Staff are really excellent and there's a pleasant little area to enjoy the sunshine or hop in the jacuzzi. Recommended.

Ponteceso and around

€€ Hostal Bahía
Av Besugueira 24, Laxe, T981 728 207,
www.bahialaxe.com.
A clean and decent year-round option if you're staying – the beach is the main reason to hang out in this town. For €20 extra, you get a room with a balcony and views.

Camariñas

There are several accommodation options in Camariñas, which gets a fair few tourists in summer. Most of them are simple, family-run *pensiones* and *hostales*; there's nothing in the luxury class.

€€ Hotel Lugar do Cotariño
T659 923 693, www.docotarino.com.
By far the best option hereabouts, this rural hotel is set in spacious grounds a couple of kilometres from Camariñas near the hamlet of Mourín. The rooms are classically modern rustic Spanish, with the exposed stone and wooden beams of the 3 old buildings artfully blended with new furniture and objets d'art.

Muxía

€€ Casa de Lema
T650 797 357, Morpeguite s/n,
www.casadelema.com.
A short way from Muxía in the hamlet of Morpeguite, this excellent *casa rural* gets plenty of repeat custom from folk that can't get enough of the pretty stone building or excellent hospitality. The rooms are exquisite for this price, with exposed stone, colourful walls, and iron-headed beds. Home-cooked meals are available for €19.

€€ **Hostal La Cruz**
Av López Abente 44, T981 742 084,
www.hostallacruz.es.
A big building with more than adequate
modern comfort and little character. The
best option in Muxía itself.

Restaurants

Ponteceso and around

€€ **Casa do Arco**
Praza Ramón Juega 1, Laxe, T981 706
904, www.casadoarco.es.
Has a good seafood restaurant.

Camariñas
There are several cafés and seafood
restaurants in Camariñas.

€€ **Gaviota**
C Río 20, T981 737 032.
Worthwhile seafood restaurant where
you just have to eat whatever's fresh
and finny that day.

What to do

Camariñas
Horse riding
If you fancy a gallop, there's a
small horse-riding operation
outside town, T981 737 279.

Sport

The city's football team, **Deportivo
La Coruña** (T902 434 443, www.
canaldeportivo.com), play their home
games at the Riazor stadium, right by
the sea. It's one of the best places in
Spain to watch a game, and the team
are notoriously difficult to beat on their
home patch. Games are normally on a
Sun evening; tickets are available from
the *taquilla* a couple of hours before the
match; you can also book by phone or
internet if you speak Spanish. Tickets
booked this way must be picked up
from a branch of Caixa Galicia bank.

Transport

Bus
Bus services run by 3 different
companies cover the Costa da Morte
thoroughly. There are at least 5 buses
daily to every destination mentioned
on this stretch of coastline. Services run
from these towns in both directions,
ie to both **A Coruña** and **Santiago**.

Towards the end of the world
beautiful windswept cape; a great spot to contemplate the setting sun

★ Fisterra and Cabo Finisterre
Further west from Cée, the town of Fisterra makes a fine place to drop anchor for
the night. It's an attractive if slightly wind-bitten fishing port, and there are plenty
of facilities catering to the passing tourists and pilgrims heading for Cabo Finisterre
a couple of kilometres beyond. There are the remains of a small fort and good views
across the bay. Fish restaurants crowd the lively waterfront, where you can visit the
important *lonja* (fish market) where the day's catch is traded. Entry costs €1.

The most westerly point in mainland Europe is not Cabo Finisterre. It's in
Portugal, and the most westerly point in Spain is a little further up the coast, but

Santiago to Cape Finisterre

A popular extension to the Camino de Santiago, and an excellent walk even if you haven't completed the pilgrimage, is the three- to four-day, 90-km walk from Santiago to the west coast. Most walkers take a short first day and a longer third day – you want to be at the cape in the late afternoon so no need to hurry.

Thus, the first day is a fairly easy walk, with not-too-onerous up-and-down stretches through pleasant pastures and light woodland, some 20 km from Santiago to the small town of Negreira, dignified by the well-known Pazo de Cotón, a curious stone mansion with medieval origins, connected to its chapel by an arch.

The next day is a rigorous one that starts with a long, steady climb of some 250 vertical metres over the course of 10 km, and then continues with rises and descents, passing through several typical Galician villages, and via viewpoints with some fine perspectives over the green countryside. Most walkers end up in Olveiroa, but there are several *albergue* options over the last stretch.

From Olveiroa, the last day – though there are several appealing places to break the walk – takes you 35 km to the end of your journey.

The first section is picturesque, following the Xallas river valley, and about halfway through the day you hit the coast at Cee. Follow on through the town of Fisterra to the cape and lighthouse at Cabo Finisterre, 2 km further along the road (a slow and often weather-beaten uphill trudge).

You can continue a further day up the coast to Muxía or, more dramatically, do this in reverse, adding an extra day from Olveiroa to Muxía, then down the coast to Fisterra from there. The trail between Muxía and Fisterra is well marked both ways. Both Fisterra and Muxía are connected to Santiago by bus several times daily.

Finisterre has won the audience vote. Part of its appeal comes from its name, derived from the Latin for 'end of the earth', part from its dramatic location: a small finger of land jutting into the mighty Atlantic. Gazing westwards from the rocks around its scruffy lighthouse (which houses a small pilgrimage exhibition) is a magical experience, particularly at sunset; imagine what it would have been like if you believed the world ended somewhere out there, dropping off into a void. The cape is 2 km uphill from Fisterra, accessible by road. There's a small bar at the top, and you can stay at the *pousada* here. In recent years, the journey from Santiago to Finisterre has become a popular extension to the pilgrimage (see box, above), and you'll likely see weary souls perched atop the cliffs, contemplating the sea at the end of their journey. Fittingly, the clifftop is marked with a cross and a sculpture of a pair of worn-out boots. Many pilgrims leave their own boots here, or burn their hiking clothes, though this is discouraged.

Carnota

Moving south again towards the Rías Baixas, the village of Carnota is set 1 km back from a magnificent and wild beach 7 km long and rolling with enormous dunes. This is one of Galicia's most spectacular coastal spots. Carnota itself has a **tourist office** at the top of town and a hotel. It also boasts the longest *hórreo* (raised granary, very typical of the region) in Galicia. The vaguely ridiculous 18th-century structure is 35 m long. You'll find it tucked away in a back street on the western side of the main road.

Listings Towards the end of the world

Where to stay

Fisterra and Cabo Finisterre
There are several pilgrim *albergues* and other budget accommodations in Fisterra.

€€€ Pousada O Semáforo
Estrada do Faro s/n, Cabo Finisterre, T981 725 869, www.osemaforo.com. Closed Nov.
Right on the headland, this is an unbeatable spot to stay. Situated in a former observatory and telegraph station, it offers considerable comfort and excellent meals (although not to the public unless previously arranged) above the wild and endless sea.

€€ Dugium
San Salvador 26, T981 740 780, www. dugium.com. Closed Oct-Easter.
In the middle of the Finisterre headland, the village of San Salvador harbours this small and peaceful rural hotel with excellent rooms, a tranquil garden and a good restaurant. Prices include breakfast.

€ Cabo Finisterre
Rúa Santa Catalina 1, Fisterra, T981 740 000. Closed Nov-Easter.
This is one of several decent *hostales* in Fisterra, with just 6 rooms and a café. Recommended.

Carnota

€ Hostal Miramar
Plaza de Galicia 2, T981 857 016, www.hostalmiramar.es.
Just off the main road in the centre of town, this is a convenient and comfortable place to stay. The rooms are well equipped and warm, with a slightly run-down beach-*hostal* feel, and there's a decent restaurant.

Restaurants

Fisterra and Cabo Finisterre
There are some excellent seafood restaurants in Fisterra.

€€€ O Centolo
Paseo del Puerto s/n, T981 740 452, www.centolo.com.
The classiest of Fisterra's restaurants, O Centolo serves an excellent range of fish and seafood in a spacious, light dining room, and also organizes dinner cruises on the bay in summer. You can eat here fairly cheaply or break the bank on the finest crustaceans. Recommended.

€€ Casa Velay
Paseo da Ribeira s/n, T981 740 127.
This place offers cordial, helpful service, and a terrace by the beach. The seafood is tops, with a generous *arroz con bogavante* (rice dish with lobster) for 2 costing €42, but it could feed a family.

Rías Baixas

The Rías Baixas are a succession of large and beautiful inlets extending down the west coast of Galicia almost as far as Portugal. The sheltered waters are used to farm much of Spain's supply of shellfish, and the towns still harbour important fishing fleets. It's one of Galicia's prime visitor destinations, a fact which has spawned a few myths that are worth clearing up. Firstly, the *rías* are not 'fjord-like' – the coast is mostly low hills, and the inlets mostly fairly shallow, retreating over mudflats at low tide. Secondly, while there are some decent beaches here, they are generally not as good as those of the Costa da Morte or north coast. Lastly, they are not remote; much of the coast is a continuous ribbon of strip development. That said, there are many spots worth visiting and much good wine and seafood to be consumed. There are also several villages and peaceful spots that merit exploration; Muros and Cambados are the most appealing bases. The region's cities, Vigo and Pontevedra, are contrasting and highly appealing centres.

unspoiled seafront town in a marvelous natural setting

The small town of Muros sits on the north coast of the northernmost *ría* of the Rías Baixas, which is named after it and Noia, its counterpart across the water. Muros has considerable charm, with a small but atmospheric old town stocked with lovely sandstone buildings, and a large fishing harbour. The Gothic church contains a Christ crucified that has a head of real hair; there's a picturesque market reached by a double staircase, and a curious stone reptile slithering over a fountain. Apart from that, it's just strolling the seafront and watching boats come and go; very pleasant indeed.

There are a few nice beaches on the Muros and Noia ría between the two towns. The blue-flag beach of **Parameán**, in the village of **Esteiro**, is one of the nicest, with clean, fine, white sand. Around **Abelleira** are another handful of good strands, with **Bornalle** one of the most inviting.

Tip...
If you fancy getting out on the water, **Costa Viva** (T686 192 031, www.cruceroscostaviva.com) runs cruises in a boat with some underwater visibility. Tapas and Galician wine are served as part of the ride.

Listings Muros

Tourist information

Muros Tourist Office
On the waterfront promenade.

Where to stay

There are several options on the waterfront road, which is often still referred to as Av Calvo Sotelo.

€€ Hotel A Muradana
Av Castelao 99, T981 826 885, www.hotelmuradana.es.
The town's smartest option is unremarkable but decent. The rooms are spacious with TV and phone; some are equipped for disabled travellers. Try for one with a sea view. There's also a restaurant and free Wi-Fi.

€€ Hotel Punta Uía
T981 855 005, www.hotelpuntauia.com.
Perched above the main road halfway between Muros and Noia, near the village of Esteiro, this attractive rural hotel offers wonderful sea views from its rooms and garden. It's a good base for hanging out on the beaches around this part of the *ría*. You pay €15 extra for a room with a balcony, but it's worth it if the weather's clement.

€€ Ría de Muros
Av Castelao 53, T981 826 056.
The most likeable place in town with a guest lounge facing the water. The best bedroom, also at the front, has a curious bedroom/bathroom annexe and is worth nabbing. Good value off season. Recommended.

€ **Hospedería A Vianda**
Av Castelao 49, T981 826 322,
www.pensionavianda.com.
Cheap but serviceable rooms above a
café/bar, which is also a great place for
a cheap *ración* or *menú del día*.

Restaurants

€€ **Casa Petra**
Av Castelao 31, T981 826 321.
A top place to try local seafood at
a decent price, this spot specializes
in generous *raciones* of octopus,
queen scallops and the like, with
some outdoor seating. Expect to
wait for a table in summer.

€ **A Dársena**
Av Castelao 11, T981 826 864.
A bright and friendly spot that does
decent pizzas and good *raciones* of *pulpo*.

Cafés

Café Theatre
In the old Mercedes theatre on the plaza.
A decent café and bar.

Camelot
C del Castillo s/n.
Built cave-like into bedrock and with
comfy seats to enjoy a drink.

Transport

Bus
There are 3 daily buses to **A Coruña**.
From just by the tourist office, buses leave
almost hourly for **Santiago via Noia**.

Noia and around

functional port town with Gothic church architecture

On the other side and further up the estuary, Noia isn't as attractive a place
as Muros, being a busier centre for the area. It's claimed that the town's name
derives from that of Noah, because this was the spot where the dove found the
olive branch; the ark came to rest on a nearby hill. Folk here believe it too, and
the event even features on the coat of arms of the town.

The Gothic **Iglesia de San Martín** is the town's highlight. Fronted by a fine *cruceiro*,
it's got an excellent carved portal featuring the Apostles, and the Elders of the
Apocalypse, and a beautiful rose window above. Another church, the **Iglesia de
Santa María** ⓘ *Mon-Sat 1000-1400, 1800-2000*, is full of the tombstones that were
salvaged from a recent clean-up of the graveyard. Rough slabs of granite dating
from the 10th to 17th centuries, they are carved with simple symbols and figures
that seem to fall into four distinct types: marks of profession, rebuses of family
names, heraldic motifs and full figures of the deceased. It's a fascinating collection.

South of Noia
Continuing south, the coast is a pretty one, with some decent, if sometimes wild-
watered, beaches. One of the better ones is **Ornanda**, just short of the decent
village of **Portosín**. At **Baroña** there is a Celtic *castro*, a fort/village well situated
on an exposed point. A couple of kilometres from the town of Axeitos down a

ON THE ROAD
Cela vida

Camilo José Cela was a hard-living author who was known in Spain as much for his flamboyant lifestyle as for his novels. Awarded the Nobel prize in 1989, Cela was a friend of Hemingway and the two shared a robust masculine approach to both life and literature.

Cela's first novel *La Familia de Pascual Duarte* (The Family of Pascual Duarte) had to be published in Argentina in 1942 because its was considered too violent and crude for Spain. The story of a murderer, its uncompromising language was unlike anything else in contemporary Spanish literature. The book inspired many imitations and was said to be the most popular Spanish novel since Cervantes. Cela published over 70 works including *La Colmena* (The Hive), a novel about the denizens of 1950s Madrid cafés and their lives and loves. The Nobel citation praised his work for its "rich and intensive prose" and its "restrained compassion."

Although he fought for the nationalists in the Civil War, Cela later published an anti-Franco magazine that became a forum for opposition to the Spanish dictator. His success as an author enabled him to pursue a lifestyle which, among other things, saw him touring his native land in a vintage Rolls Royce. He died in 2002.

peaceful country lane is one of the nicer of Galicia's many **dolmens**; it sits in a dappled glade among pine cones. Near here a winding road leads up to a mirador, **La Curota**. If the day is good, the view is absolutely breathtaking, taking in all the *rías*, with their shellfish platforms looking like squadrons of U-boats in harbour. You can see north to Finisterre and south to Baiona, just short of Portugal.

Santa Uxía de Ribeira (usually just called Ribeira or Riveira) is the main town in this region, an important fishing port and popular tourist destination. There are fabulous views over the wide bay with its rocky islets; what's left of the old town clusters behind the fishing harbour, but the major attraction is the fine deep sheltered beach, Playa Coroso, a short walk from the centre. This is the beginning of the next inlet, the **Ría de Arousa**, the largest of this coast. **Cambados** is the most attractive place to stay on this *ría*.

Listings Noia and around

Tourist information

Noia Tourist Office
Opposite the town hall, T981 842 100, Mon-Fri 1030-1300, Sat and Sun 1200-
1300 (extended opening in Jul and Aug).
The kiosk is built around a small, attractive atrium.

Where to stay

€€ Elisardo
Costa do Ferrador 15, T981 820 130.
Near the shallows of the *ría* with good,
clean rooms with bathroom. It's modern
in feel and welcoming in style and offers
decent value, even in summer, when you
should book as there are only a handful
of rooms. Good cheap restaurant.

€€ La Pesquería del Tambre
*Central do Tambre, Santa María
de Roo, T981 051 620, www.
pesqueriadeltambre.com.*
Northeast of Noia, along a winding
road off the Santiago highway, this
former hydroelectric station has been
transformed into a sensational rustic
hotel. It's a secluded spot, with rooms
spread out among different buildings in
a picturesque riverside location. There's a
pool and restaurant, and utter relaxation.
Stay a few days. Recommended.

Restaurants

€€ Mesón Senra
Rúa Escultor Ferreiro 18, T981 820 084.
A characterful restaurant that relies on
its typically cosy Galician decor of stone
and wood, and sterling service and
food. The excellent *zamburiñas* (queen
scallops) will satisfy parts other seafoods
don't reach, while the sardines (*xoubas*
in Galicia) are also bursting with flavour.
There are appealing outdoor tables
under the stone arches.

Transport

Bus
Hourly buses to **Santiago** and **Muros**.

Padrón

famous for its peppers and literary connections

A busy road junction, Padrón at first glance seems unappealing, but it has several interesting associations. It was a Roman town, and tradition has it that the followers of Saint James landed here after bringing his body back from Palestine. The parish church by the bridge over the river displays *el pedrón* (mooring-stone) under the altar. The small but picturesque old town is a relief to stroll in, away from the busy road.

Padrón is also famous for its peppers, which have DO (*denominación de origen*) status; the small, green *pimientos de Padrón* are mild, slightly sweet and are seen all over Spain. They are typically cooked in hot oil. Although most are harmless, the odd one is famously fiery; the Spaniards have a saying: '*O los pimientos de Padrón: unos pican, y otros no*' (Oh, the peppers of Padrón: some of them bite and some of them don't).

Padrón also has a strong literary connection. It was the long-time home of Galicia's favourite poet, Rosalía de Castro (see box, page 26). Her pretty gardened house has been turned into a museum, the **Casa Museo de Rosalía** ⓘ *www. rosaliadecastro.org, Tue-Sat 1000-1330, 1600-1900 (closes 1400 and 2000 in summer), Sun 1000-1330, €2*, opposite the station. In it are various personal possessions and biographical notes. Padrón's other writer, the Nobel prize-winning novelist Camilo

José Cela (see box, page 70) was born on the town's outskirts. A former **canon's residence** has been turned into a museum displaying various manuscripts of his work and personal possessions, including a yellowing newspaper collection. Across the road is the collegiate **Iglesia de Santa María de Iria Flavia**, where the writer was baptized; it claims to have been the first church dedicated to Mary in the world (and therefore marks the beginning of Spanish polytheism).

Listings Padrón

Tourist information

There's a small **tourist kiosk** on the main road.

Where to stay

€€ Hotel Jardín
Rúa Salgado Araujo 3, T981 810 950, www.pensionjardin.com.
This is a great little spot to stay, which offers excellent value in a big modernized 18th-century stone house shaded by palm trees and by the Jardín Botánico. There's some traffic noise from the main road.

Restaurants

€€€ A Casa dos Martínez
Plaza Baltar 7, T981 810 577.
In the heart of the picturesque old part of town, this discreet, upmarket place offers imaginatively prepared and presented modern takes on traditional Galician cuisine and politely formal service. The local peppers (*pimientos de Padrón*) are delicious. The set *menú* includes a decent choice of wines.

€€€ Chef Rivera
Enlace Parque 7, T981 810 523, www.chefrivera.com.
The finest spot in town. Sitting under the hotel of the same name, this uses the best of Galician ingredients. The lampreys are great, the octopus sublime and the wine list mighty impressive. Prices are very fair.

€ Os Carrisos
C Calvo Sotelo 27, www.oscarrisos.com.
On the main road through town, this excellent traditional *pulpería* has an airy front dining area and a rustic bar where you can drink ribeiro wine and enjoy delicious *raciones* of octopus.

Transport

Bus and train
Regular connections with **Santiago**.

Villagarcía de Arousa and around

functional holiday town; a decent base for exploring the area

Villagarcía de Arousa is one of the wealthier towns on this stretch of coast, with its fair share of urbanizations and brash modern villas. It's an important fishing port, but the cash here wasn't just the result of a bumper prawn harvest; seafood of a more lucrative, Colombian variety traditionally found its way ashore around here in notable quantities.

It's an easygoing, uncomplicated sort of town, filled with holidaymakers in summer, and doesn't make a bad base for a relaxed exploration of the coast. A quieter and more appealing option can be found just to the north in **O Carril**, a pretty fishing harbour with several top-quality restaurants; there's also an excellent beach nearby, **Praia Compostela**, although you won't have it to yourself in summer.

Illa de Arousa

South of Vilagarcía, Illa de Arousa is an island linked to the mainland by a long modern bridge. It's relatively unspoiled, although not especially scenic. The main town, also known as Illa de Arousa or Xufre, is a small fishing port. The beaches are sheltered and pleasant enough, although they're not blessed with acres of white sand. The southern half of the island also preserves some important waterbird habitats.

Listings Villagarcía de Arousa

Tourist information

Villagarcía de Arousa Tourist Office
On the waterfront promenade where the buses stop, T986 501 008, turismo@vilagarcia.es. Mon-Sat 1000-1300, 1630-1830 (2000 summer), Sun summer only 1000-1400.

Where to stay

€€€ Pazo O Rial
El Rial 1, T986 507 011, www.pazorial.com.
Just south of Vilagarcía, on the shoulder of a ridge, this hillside *pazo* (country mansion) in a walled garden off the main road is one of the best places on this coast. It's well priced with attentive service and atmosphere, and it's even got a long *hórreo* and its own *cruceiro*. Recommended.

€€ Playa Compostela
Av Rosalía de Castro 134, O Carril, T986 504 010, www.galinor.es/playacompostela.
A modern hotel replete with facilities. Rooms are bright and clean, and

it's excellent value year round. Recommended.

Illa da Arousa

€ Hotel Benalúa
Rúa Méndez Núñez s/n, T986 551 332.
The only hotel on the island, this is no luxury choice, but is simple and cheap.

Camping

Salinas
T986 527 444, www.campingsalinas.com. Jun-Sep.
The campsite with the most facilities.

Restaurants

€€€ Loliña
Praza Muelle s/n, O Carril, T986 501 281.
The best place to eat hereabouts, this restaurant is a superb ivy-swathed place with characterful Gallego decor. The house speciality is *rape* (monkfish/anglerfish).

€€ Casa Bóveda
Paseo La Mariña 2, O Carril, T986 511 204, www.restaurantecasaboveda.com.

This is similarly good. They do a delicious *arroz con bogavante*, a rice dish sizzling away with pieces of lobster aboard.

Transport

Bus
Hourly buses from **Santiago** and **Pontevedra** to Vilagarcía de Arousa.

Illa da Arousa
Bus
Buses from **Pontevedra** visit the island a couple of times a day, otherwise it's not too far to walk across to the mainland, where buses along the main road are frequent.

Cambados and around
exquisite old town, famous for its Albariño wine

★Cambados
This noble old town is by far the nicest place to stay on this *ría*, and indeed perhaps on the whole of the Rías Baixas. The highlight is the huge granite-paved square, flanked by impressive buildings and an archway, and only slightly marred by the cars zipping across it. Other attractive houses line the narrow lanes of the town. The crumbling **Iglesia de Santa Mariña de Dozo** is now used as a cemetery; its 12th-century ruins are an atmospheric place.

Cambados is also the centre of the Rías Baixas wine region, which has DO (*denominación de origen*) status. Most of the land under vines is given over to the Albariño grape, which produces highly aromatic whites, fruity and flowery but crisp-finished, reminiscent of dry German wines; indeed, one theory of the variety's origin is that Benedictine monks brought it to the region from the Rhine. It tends to be made in small quantities, and is comparatively pricey but a great match with the region's shellfish. You can learn all about it in the **Museo Etnográfico del Vino** ① *Av Pastora 104, T986 526 119, Tue-Sat 1000-1400, 1630-1900, Sun 1000-1400, Jun-Oct afternoon opening 1700-2000, €3.20*, a wine museum divided between two connected buildings near the Santa Mariña de Dozo church. Entry includes admission to a couple of other museums in town, including a small display of wine routes. Of several bodegas in the area, one of the finest is **Martín Códax** ① *5 km east of town, T986 524 499, www.martincodax.com; it's open for visits by prior appointment Mon-Fri 1100-1300, 1600-2000*. In the centre of town, behind a narrow park. **Expo Salnés** ① *T986 521 008, Mon-Fri 1000-1400, 1700-2000*, is a tourist board-style exhibition about this area of the Rías Baixas and also functions as the town's tourist office. On the first Sunday in August, Cambados celebrates its wine industry with the boisterous Festa do Albariño, well worth the trip if you're in the area.

O Grove
The resort town of O Grove enjoys an excellent natural setting at the tip of a peninsula at the southern mouth of the *ría*. No doubt it was once a charming fishing port, but it is fairly developed these days. Still, it's a cheerful and likeable place and could make a good venue for a relaxed waterside family holiday, with its large

number of hotels, outdoor activities and seafood eateries. There are numerous fine beaches within a short drive from town. There's a **tourist information kiosk** ⓘ *T986 731 415*, near the fish *lonja* by the water in the heart of town. Next to it is a large statue of a shell-fishing couple, one of dozens of public sculptures that decorate the town centre.

The most interesting sight in the area is the **O Grove aquarium** ⓘ *T986 731 515, www.acuariodeogrove.es, mid-Jun to mid-Oct 1030-2030 daily, mid-Oct to mid-Jun Wed-Fri 1000-1800, Sat-Sun 1030-2030, adult/child €10/8*, 5 km to the west near the village of **Reboredo**. Recently remodelled and reopened, it's of most interest for its detailed coverage of the sealife of the *rías* and North Atlantic.

The area around O Grove is also good for watching waterbirds; many species can be seen patrolling the muddy edges of the *ría*. The main focus for life in the town is the waterfront promenade. Several companies run hourly glass-bottomed boat excursions from here in summer. The trips take about 1½ hours and cost around €15 per head. There's most to be seen on and around the shellfish-breeding platforms, and the trip includes a tasting.

A Toxa

It's a sobering thought that A Toxa was described by Georges Pillement in just 1964 as "an earthly paradise". A lover of getting off the beaten track, the French writer would be appalled at his little island now. It's linked to O Grove by a short bridge, and although it's still attractively wooded, most of the atmosphere has been removed by the construction of several no-holds-barred luxury spa hotels (the thermal waters here are said to be beneficial), ugly apartments and a casino. If you can dodge the old women selling seashells, stroll around the western half of the island, which is still fragrant with pine. Otherwise, while the hotels lack no comforts, the island is an overpriced disappointment.

Praia A Lanzada

The best beach around this region is Praia A Lanzada, on the seaward side of the narrow neck of the peninsula. Its an excellent sandy stretch whose waters are said to boost female fertility. There's a small chapel at the southern end of the beach; a prayer and a dip are the traditional alternative to IVF in these parts. It's most effective on the night of the 23 June, with the moon shining. The swim must last exactly nine waves.

Sanxenxo

The resort of Sanxenxo lies on the northern edge of the Ría de Pontevedra and is something of a focus for the area's nightlife. The nicest bit of it is its high headland, while the waterfront is packed with cafés and bars. It's also a watersports centre, and makes a cheerful seaside base conveniently close to the cities of Pontevedra and Vigo. There's a boat service from Sanxenxo to the beautiful island of Ons (see Pontevedra to Vigo, page 80).

€€€ Parador de Cambados
Paseo de Cervantes s/n, T986 542 250,
www.parador.es.
In the heart of town, this fine place
set in a traditional Galician *pazo*
(country mansion) has a good garden
and rooms. There's a pool, tennis court,
and pretty patio.

€€ Casa Mariñeira Lourdes
Av Pastora 95, T986 543 985,
www.cmlourdes.net.
The nicest of several *casas rurales*, this
one has big very homely bedrooms
and offers more than decent value.
Some rooms share a bathroom and are
significantly cheaper. The owners also
have rental apartments in the village.

€€ Hotel Real Ribadomar
Rua Real 8, T986 524 404,
www.hotelrealribadomar.com.
This modern boutique hotel is situated
right in the heart of Cambados and has a
variety of distinct, beautifully decorated
rooms with appealing bathrooms.
Service is polite and efficient.

€ Hostal Pazos Feijóo
Rúa Curros Enríquez 1, T986 542 810.
A decent and centrally located *hostal* in
the southern part of town, with a friendly
owner. Rooms are simple but spacious,
with spotless en suite bathrooms.

O Grove and A Toxa
There are so many hotels that getting
a room is never a problem, even in
summer, although finding a bargain
is trickier.

€€€€ Gran Hotel La Toja
Isla de la Toxa, T986 730 025,
www.granhotellatoja.com.
The top hotel in the area, on the
secluded enclave of A Toxa. It's got the
lot, including a golf course, pools, gym
and sauna, and anything else you care
to name.

€€ Hostal María Aguiño
Rúa de Pablo Iglesias 26, T986 733 007,
www.hospedaxemariaaguino.com.
A friendly option offering good value,
a couple of streets from the waterfront,
right in the heart of things.

€€ Hotel Maruxia
C Luis Casais 14, T986 732 795,
www.hotelmaruxia.com.
This is a reasonable choice and open
all year-round – out of season its clean
and proper double rooms come down
substantially in value, but it's not badly
priced for the zone in summer.

Praia A Lanzada

€€ Hotel Nuevo La Lanzada
T986 743 232, www.hoteleslanzada.com.
Mar-Oct.
This is a more than decent beachfront
hotel with fine clean and bright rooms,
some with balcony and views; there's
also a restaurant. The sister hotel here is
a little older but still decent; the prices
are the same and it has a restaurant.
Minimum 3-night stay in high summer.

Camping

Cachadelos
*T986 745 592, www.camping
cachadelos.com. Apr–Sep.*
The best equipped of 3 summer
campsites, with a pool and
wooden bungalows.

Sanxenxo
There are dozens of hotels here and
along this stretch of coast.

€€€ Gran Talaso Hotel Sanxenxo
*Paseo de Silgar 3, T986 691 111,
www.hotelsanxenxo.com.*
This large spa hotel has excellent
facilities, and pleasing rooms, most
with sea views (these cost a little more).
There are good off-season rates, and
various packages combining your stay
with meals, spa treatments, etc. There's
also an outdoor pool. A minimum stay
applies in summer.

€€ Antiga Casa de Reis
*Reis 39, T986 690 550,
www.antigacasadereis.com.*
In the hills just behind Sanxenxo, this
luxurious *casa rural* is one of the best
of its kind in this part of the world. The
thoughtfully decorated rooms have
various artfully chosen curios and noble
rustic furnishings, but are spacious and
uncluttered. The breakfasts are delicious,
and the hosts helpful and charming.
Recommended.

€€ Casa Román
*Rúa Carlos Casas 2, T986 720 031,
www.casaroman.com.*
A moderately priced option in Sanxenxo
itself, with comfortably simple en suite
rooms that are pretty good value for this
coastline. Breakfast is included.

€€ Casa Zulema
*Arra/Playa Montalvo s/n, T986 691 991,
www.casazulema.com.*
A reader-recommended spot about 1 km
from the beach in Portonovo, west of
Sanxenxo, this has correct and clean rooms
at a reasonable price, and no-frills but tasty
traditional dishes in the bar-restaurant.

Restaurants

€€ María José
Paseo de Cervantes s/n, T986 542 281.
A loveable 1st-floor restaurant opposite
the parador – the quality of the food is
above and beyond what you'd expect
for this price; just go with the staff
recommendations. Recommended.

€€ Posta do Sol
Ribeira de Fefiñans 22, T986 542 285.
A good seafood restaurant housed
in a traditional former bar.

O Grove and A Toxa
The waterfront in O Grove bristles with
seafood restaurants, nearly all of which
range from good to excellent. It's difficult
to go wrong here, but be careful ordering
things by weight, as bills can add up fast.

€€ Beiramar
*Paseo Marítimo 28, T986 731 081, www.
restaurantebeiramar.com. Closed Nov.*
Another of the best-established of the
fishy eating choices, this has excellent
presentation and acceptable service in
a comfortably attractive dining room.

Sanxenxo

€€ O Forno
Seixalvo 25, T618 372 603.
It's worth seeking out this restaurant
on the hill behind town for its excellent
Galician cuisine at generous prices.

Pontevedra, Vigo
& south to Portugal

It's hard to imagine two more contrasting cities than Pontevedra and Vigo, yet both are enchanting. The former is a petite, genteel sort of place, with a picturesque old town studded with gorgeous plazas, while the latter is a big, heart-on-sleeve blue-collar sprawl, a fishing city par excellence, situated on a spectacular bay. South of here, Baiona is one of Galicia's most appealing seaside towns, and the Celtic settlement above A Guarda stares across the Miño at Portugal, stone foundations still growling defiantly.

Pontevedra and around

small but lively provincial capital buzzing with history and culture

In contrast to its overdeveloped *ría*, Pontevedra is a charming place; its beautiful old centre and relaxed street life make it a top town to visit. It's the most attractive spot in which to base yourself to explore the Rías Baixas; its good bus and train connections make day trips an easy prospect. Its only downside is the occasionally nostril-searing odour from the massive paper mill a couple of kilometres down the *ría*.

Sights

Pontevedra's endearing old town is built mostly of granite, and preserves a real medieval feel around its network of postcard-pretty plazas and stone colonnades. Perhaps the nicest of the squares is the small, irregular **Praza da Leña**, ringed by attractive houses. Like many of the plazas, it contains a *cruceiro*. The bigger **Praza da Verdura** nearby is another good space with arcades and coats of arms on some of the grander buildings.

Around the large, social **Praza da Ferrería** are two churches, the curiously rounded, domed **Santuario de la Virgen Peregrina**, where pilgrims on their way to Santiago on the *Camino Portugués* traditionally drop in; and the larger **Igrexa de San Francisco**, with some attractive stained glass, carved tombs of goggle-eyed nobles and a fine rose window, as well as an array of saints, pleasingly including some of the less-commonly venerated stalwarts of the church.

The **Basílica de Santa María a Maior** ⓘ *Mon-Sat 1000-1300, Sun 1000-1400, 1800-2100, free*, is Pontevedra's finest church, which looks especially attractive when bathed in the evening sun. Dating mostly from the 16th century, it has particularly elaborate ribbed vaulting, late Gothic arches, a dark *retablo* that predates the church, and a sloping floor. The fine Plateresque façade is the work of a Flemish master and depicts scenes from the life of the Virgin Mary. In the

Pontevedra

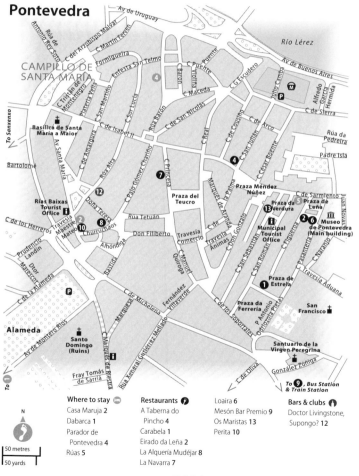

Where to stay 🛏	Restaurants 🍴	Loaira 6	Bars & clubs 🎵
Casa Maruja 2	A Taberna do	Mesón Bar Premio 9	Doctor Livingstone,
Dabarca 1	Pincho 4	Os Maristas 13	Supongo? 12
Parador de	Carabela 1	Perita 10	
Pontevedra 4	Eirado da Leña 2		
Rúas 5	La Alquería Mudéjar 8		
	La Navarra 7		

N

50 metres
50 yards

BACKGROUND
Pontevedra

Like several inland Galician towns, Pontevedra was formerly an important seaport but was left stranded by its river, which deposited large quantities of silt into the *ría*, handing Vigo the initiative for maritime activity. It's said that Pontevedra was founded by Trojan colonists that left the Mediterranean after the defeat by the Greeks; though there's little evidence, it doesn't even come close to being the tallest of the tall stories along this coast. Pontevedra declined in the 17th and 18th centuries, but on being appointed capital of this economically important Galician province a measure of wealth returned, and it's now a fairly prosperous administrative centre with a population of 81,576. Its proximity to Vigo means that many people commute between the two cities.

gardens on the old town side of the church is a stone marking the location of the old Jewish cemetery.

The **Museo de Pontevedra** ① *www.museo.depo.es, Tue-Sat 1000-2100, Sun 1100-1400, free to EU passport holders, otherwise €1.20 (they don't tend to check)*, covers five separate buildings, with the main one on Praza da Leña. It's one of the better such museums in Spain's north; the Celtic jewellery is a definite highlight; there's also a large 19th-century silverware collection and a replica of a 19th-century Spanish frigate admiral's onboard quarters. Some good paintings are present, including works by Goya and Zurbarán among many Galician, Aragonese and Catalan artists. One of the museum's buildings is the atmospheric, ruined **Iglesia de Santo Domingo** by the Alameda; it contains a number of tombstones from different historical periods.

Pontevedra to Vigo

Moving southwards along the coast from Pontevedra, the reeking paper mill makes the first few kilometres unattractive, although the cheery maritime murals on the factory are at least a token effort. There's a large naval academy at the small port of **Marín**, and near Mogor are some important Celtic stone carvings. Both Marín and the nearby town of **Bueu** are points of departure for summer excursions to the beautiful and peaceful **Isla de Ons**, one of four island groups that make up the national park of Islas Atlánticas de Galicia, in a glass-bottomed catamaran (T986 320 048, www.isladeons.net). The boats make the crossing daily from July to September. You can reserve the island's campsite at www.iatlanticas.es. There's also a hotel and restaurant on the island, whose details are on the same website; it pays to reserve rooms well in advance. It's a rugged, rustic place, so don't expect luxury: electricity is limited to lunchtimes and evenings.

Hío One of the nicest places on this stretch is the village of Hío, on the headland that divides the *rías* of Pontevedra and Vigo; it's 1 km from the main road. Its church has a Romanesque portal, but the highlight is its *cruceiro* out the front, an intricate work carved almost wholly from a single block of granite. At the top is a Crucifixion of some emotion, below is a scene of Mary helping sinners in Purgatory, while Adam and Eve stand bashfully underneath. An angel watches the scenes from another pillar nearby. It's one of the finest *cruceiros* of Galicia, although certainly not the oldest, being sculpted in 1872. There's a small tourist information kiosk nearby. The village itself is a pleasant spot, and there are some very good beaches around the headland.

Cangas Cangas is a busy little seaside resort and satellite of Vigo, with some good bars on the waterfront as well as a pretty little chapel. There's a regular ferry across to Vigo used by commuters; it's the smart option, as the traffic between here and there is terrible. Cangas was a hotbed of witchcraft in the 17th century, at least according to those loveable chaps of the Inquisition. Much of the unorthodox behaviour that caused concern could perhaps be attributed to post-traumatic symptoms; the town was viciously sacked by Barbary corsairs shortly before, leaving much of the population dead. If you prefer to stay here to Vigo, see Where to stay, page 82. Moaña, a little closer to Vigo, also has a ferry service, and is a bit quieter.

Listings Pontevedra and around *map p79*

Tourist information

There are 3 tourist offices in Pontevedra.

Galician regional tourist office
Just outside the old town, Rúa Marqués de Riestra 30, T986 850 814, oficina. turismo.pontevedra@xunta.es. Winter Mon-Fri 1000-1400, 1600-1800, Sat 1000-1230, summer Mon-Fri 1000-1400, 1630-1930, Sat 1000-1400, 1630-1930, Sun 1000-1400.

Municipal information office
In the heart of the old town, Pr da Verdura s/n, T986 090 890, www.visit-pontevedra. com. Daily 0900-1330, 1600-1930.

Rías Baixas office
Pr de Santa María s/n, T986 211 700, www.riasbaixas.depo.es. Summer Mon-Fri 0900-2100, Sat-Sun 1000-1430, 1630-2000, earlier closing winter.
Provides information on this section of coastline and the offshore islands.

Where to stay

€€ Hotel Dabarca
Rúa de los Palamios 2, T986 869 723, www.hoteldabarca.com.
This new-town hotel is a great option for a family holiday, offering handsome, spacious apartments with kitchen and washing machine.

€€ Hotel Rúas
C Figueroa 35, T986 846 416, www.hotelruas.net.
You can't beat the location of this hotel, in the liveliest area of the beautiful centre, set right between 2 of the prettiest plazas. The rooms have large comfortable beds and are very good for the price; the showers are gloriously powerful. There's a café downstairs and a warm welcome. It's much cheaper off season. Recommended.

€€ **Parador de Pontevedra**
Rúa Barón 19, T986 855 800,
www.parador.es.
This lovely parador is in the heart of the
old town, set in a *palacio* on a pretty
square. There's a beautiful garden and
terrace, and the rooms are decorated
with style and comfort.

€ **Casa Maruja**
Av Santa María 2, T986 854 901.
Good, cheap, ageing rooms, clean and
with TV; some en suite. It's very well
located in the old town.

Pontevedra to Vigo

€€ **Hotel Airiños**
Rúa da Marina s/n, Cangas, T986 340
000, www.airinos.com.
A decent option on the boulevard.
Rooms are comfortably spacious if
darkish. It's worth paying a little extra for
larger ones with a sea view and lounge
area. It's € off-season.

€€ **Hotel Playa**
Av de Ourense 78, Cangas.
T986 303 674, www.hotel-playa.com.
Slightly cheaper than the Airiños and a
short way east of the main bustle but
right on the beach and a good choice for
families. Rooms are clean and bright.

Restaurants

There are characterful, traditional
tapas and wine bars along C Isabel
II and C Princesa in the old centre.
Numerous terraces to eat on crowd
the plazas in summer.

€€€ **Casa Solla**
Av Sineiro 7, San Salvador de Poyo, T986
873 198, www.restaurantesolla.com.
An excellent Galician restaurant with
innovative molecular gastronomy dishes,

5 km west of Pontevedra on the way to
Sanxenxo. It's often considered to offer
the region's best modern Spanish cuisine,
best sampled on the exquisite 12-course
degustation menu. The setting, in a
noble mansion surrounded by garden,
matches the high quality of the food.

€€€ **Eirado da Leña**
Praza da Leña 1, T986 860 225.
On Pontevedra's prettiest square, this
has a coolly elegant interior and a sunny
terrace for convivial lunching among the
combined chatter of competing alfresco
eateries. Well-prepared fish dishes are
the signature here, and there are several
set menu options allowing you to try a
range of morsels.

€€ **Loaira**
Praza da Leña 2, T986 858 815.
Run by an enthusiastic young couple,
this tiny corner place expands on to the
square outside in summer. Good fresh
salads and other brightly presented
raciones are on offer, and there's a
reasonably priced lunch *menú*.

€€ **Mesón Bar Premio**
Rúa da Peregrina 29, T986 103 528.
This atmospheric spot is a godsend if
you are lugging heavy bags from the
bus station into the old town on a hot
day. A tapa of the delicious ham and a
glass of something cold and you'll be
on your way again with renewed vigour.
It's also a great spot to sit down and eat
and decorated in the traditional manner
with venerable wine bottles and
hanging *charcutería*.

€ **A Taberna do Pincho**
Praza Méndez Núñez 15, T986 857 840.
A popular meeting point in the heart of
Pontevedra. You'll get a small free snack
with your drink, and there's also a wide
choice of nibbles or more substantial fare

such as *revueltos*, which you can eat at the downstairs tables. There's a cheap lunchtime *menú*.

€ Bar os Maristas
Praza da Verdura 5, T986 844 075.
Another old-fashioned place, this is as authentic as it comes, with old men drinking their pre-lunch wines out of traditional white ceramic crucibles. There are cheap *raciones* of very tasty traditional Galician fare and a terrace in summer.

€ La Alquería Mudéjar
Rúa Churruchaos 2, T986 851 258.
With wooden tables, yellow lighting and a convivial buzz, this is a place to lift the spirits. There's a fine selection of wines and plenty of simple *raciones* and dishes. The *tortilla* is great, as are the brochettes; this is a real enclave of genuine hospitality. Recommended.

€ La Navarra
C Princesa 13, T986 851 254.
Traditional with a capital T, this no-frills bar and wine shop serves up wine and traditional Galician fare in a great atmosphere. It's one of several old-time bars worth exploring on this street and Isabel II, which intersects it.

Cafés

Carabela
Praza da Estrela 1, T986 851 215.
A famous café with a relaxing outdoor terrace on the largest square, where you can watch Pontevedra's children feeding or chasing the pigeons.

Perita
Corner of Av Santa María and C Churruchaos.
Serving as both café and night-time bar, this stylish venue is squeezed into an attractive stone space and given a modern feel with its underlit shelves, sleek bar and contemporary art exhibited on the walls. The coffee is excellent and comes with a little pastry; the *copas* are also well poured.

Pontevedra to Vigo

€€€ Laurel
Ctra del Muelle s/n, San Adrián de Cobres, Vilaboa, T986 672 581, www.restaurantelaurel.es.
This top option just off the main road between Vigo and Pontevedra boasts a crisp, modern dining room with great sea views, located right over the water in the Vilaboa yacht club. They use top-quality local products to create innovative, beautifully presented contemporary dishes. Faultless. Recommended.

Bars and clubs

Praza del Teucro is the old-town centre for evening drinking. After hours the *marcha* moves out a little; many people head for Sanxenxo in summer, or the town of Arcade, 5 km south, which has, as well as a number of *marisquerías*, several bars and *discotecas* along its main street, C Castelao.

Doctor Livingstone Supongo?
Rúa Alta 4.
A rhino and an elephant stare you down as you approach the door of this café and bar that's a Pontevedra favourite for *copas*.

Entertainment

Pontevedra has a good cultural programme; look out for the monthly guide in the tourist office.

Teatro Principal, *Rúa Charino 6, T986 851 932.*

Transport

Bus
Pontevedra's bus station is a 20-min walk southeast of the town centre on Rúa da Peregrina. **Ourense** is served 8 times a day, **A Coruña** about 10 times, and **Santiago** (50 mins) even more frequently. There are hourly buses to **O Grove**, and even more to **Sanxenxo**. 10 per day go to **Cangas** and buses leave every 30 mins or so for **Vigo** (some to the bus station, some to the waterfront, 25 mins). 2 a day go to **Padrón** and **Noia**, and 4 to **Tui** and **Valença** (Portugal). Hourly buses head north to **Vilagarcía**, some taking in the island of **Illa Arousa**, and 8 go to **Cambados**. 6 buses cross Galicia to **Lugo** every day.

There are 2 long-distance buses to **Madrid**, 2 to **Bilbao** via Oviedo or Burgos, 1 or 2 to **Barcelona** and **Zaragoza**, 1 to **Salamanca**, **Gijón**, and **Valladolid**. There are many more routes from nearby Vigo.

Train
The train station is next to the bus station. There are frequent connections to **Vigo** (33 mins) and **A Coruña** (1½ hrs) via **Santiago**.

Vigo

large industrial city with a magnificent estuary setting

Vigo, with a population of 297,355, is Galicia's largest city (the fourth largest in Northern Spain), and the world's second largest fishing port by volume (after Toyko), supplying huge quantities of sardines, among other things, to the whole of Europe. With a beautiful location spread along its wide bay, it's a curiously divided place. The old part of town is a working port and wholly down-to-earth. Traffic problems, urban decay and poverty are all present and evident, but it still recalls its golden days as an important steamer port bustling with passengers bound for London, Portugal and South America. Faded but proud old buildings line the streets descending to the harbour, and the fresh seafood on offer here is as good as anywhere in Europe. By contrast, the newer zone around the marina is full of trendy cafés and waterfront promenades. If you're looking for a quiet, restful stop you may hate Vigo; if you're the sort of person who finds busy ports and earthy sailors' bars a little romantic it's an intriguing and likeable place.

Sights
Vigo's main sight is its busy **waterfront**. There are kilometres of it to wander if you're so inclined, and even the commercial docks are mostly easily accessible. Right in the centre is the passenger terminal where steamers used to dock; next to it is where the ferries leave for the ports of **Cangas** and **Moaña** across the bay, as well as the **Islas Cíes** in summer. The terminal still gets the odd cruise ship in, and lots of yachts still put in at the marina just east of here, which is backed with all manner of trendy bars and restaurants.

To the west of the passenger terminal, it's worth having a look at the fishing port, where boats of all sizes and nationalities drop in on their way to and from the

Atlantic fisheries. Further round are repair docks and shipwrecking yards, and the **Puerto de Bouzas** beyond is the customs-bonded dock where commercial goods are unloaded. When the fishing boats come in at dawn, *marisqueiras* (typically the wives of the fishermen) still sell fresh shellfish (the oysters are delicious) around the streets; particularly on the covered **Rúa da Pescadería** near the marina, popularly known as Calle de las Ostras, or Oyster Street.

The main attraction in the town itself is the elegant architecture on the streets leading back from the passenger terminal, very faded but a poignant reminder of golden days. Just to the west, the narrow streets are the oldest part of the town; it's known as **Berbés**, and is full of little watering-holes and eateries. It has its vaguely seedy side but is on the up again, with boutiques, trendy bars and worthwhile fish restaurants.

The **Museo do Mar de Galicia** ① *Av Atlántida 160, T986 247 750, www.museodomar.com, mid-Jun to mid-Sep Tue-Fri 1100-1400, 1700-2000, Sat-Sun 1100-2100, mid-Sep to mid-Jun Tue-Fri 1000-1400, Sat-Sun 1100-1900, €3*, is a modern museum on the waterfront a fair way west of the centre. It's an interesting display of Spanish maritime history and includes an exhibition on the treasure fleet

Vigo

Where to stay
AC Palacio Universal **1**
Aguila **4**
Compostela **2**
Hostal Buenos Aires **7**
Infinnit **8**
La Nueva Colegiata **5**
Puerta de Gamboa **6**
Puerta del Sol **3**

Restaurants
Bitácora **1**
Casa Esperanza **3**
Don Quijote **5**
El Mosquito **7**
Jackie's **2**
La Trastienda del 4 **8**
Mesón El Capitán **9**
Vinoteca Cabernet **6**

Bars & clubs
Iguana Club **3**
La Abadía de Santos **10**
Uno Está **8**

200 metres
200 yards

BACKGROUND

Vigo

Vigo's top natural harbour was used by the Phoenicians and Celts before the city as we know it was founded by the Romans, who named it Vicus Spacorum. Vigo's curse was often its pretty offshore islands, the Islas Cíes, which were used throughout history as cover and a supply base for a series of swashbucklers, raiders and pirates, including Vikings, Corsairs and Britons; Sir Francis Drake spent a couple of years menacing Vigo on a regular basis. In 1702 a passing British fleet of only 25 ships heard that the treasure fleet from South America was in the port with a French escort. Their surprise attack was a success; they sank 20 and captured 11 of the fleet. The gold and silver was still on board because at that time only Cádiz had official permission to unload bullion from the colonies. Rumour has it that most of it was dumped into the sea; numerous diving expeditions have been mounted over the last couple of centuries, but no success had been reported. In the late 19th century, as the golden age of the steamer began, Vigo grew massively and became prosperous on the back of this and increasingly efficient fishing methods; nearly all its public buildings date from 1860 to 1890. Decline set in in the 20th century, particularly during the stultifying Franco years, when Spain lagged far behind other European powers, but later large manufacturing plants, such as the huge Peugeot-Citröen operation, brought much employment to the city. Pontevedra's status as provincial capital continues to annoy Vigo (until the new standardized numberplates came in, locals used to travel to far-away Vitoria so their car would bear the 'VI'); there has never been much love lost between the two cities, and locals feel their city doesn't get a fair slice of the pie from the provincial administration. Nevertheless, the local administration is making a big effort at urban renewal, including rehabilitation of the central barrios and the installing of a fine series of modern sculpture all around town, and little by little Vigo is beginning to recover the sparkle that its superb natural setting deserves.

disaster of 1702 and the importance of trade with the New World colonies. There's also an aquarium (€2) focusing on the local marine ecosystem.

The **Museo Municipal Quiñones de León** ⓘ *www.museodevigo.org, Tue-Fri 1000-1400, Sat 1700-2000, Sun 1100-1400, free*, is a museum in an old Galician mansion in the Parque de Castrelos south of the centre; it has period furniture and a decent collection of Galician paintings and makes a peaceful retreat from Vigo's working centre. In an adjacent annex is a reasonable archaeological collection.

★Islas Cíes

The offshore Islas Cíes are a complete contrast to Vigo and the overdeveloped *rías*; an unspoilt (though much-visited) natural paradise, uninhabited and only visitable in summer. The area is comprised of three main islands (two of which are connected), rocky and rugged, and harbouring quiet coves with wonderfully romantic white sand beaches once the haunt of pirates. It is one of the archipelagos that make up the **Islas Atlánticas National Park**. In summer (mid-June to mid-September), ferries run to the islands from the passenger dock; you'll have to return the same day unless you simultaneously purchase a voucher for the **campsite** ⓘ *T986 438 358, T986 225 582 in winter, www.campingislascies.com*, which has a shop and bar/restaurant. There are four boats a day, and a return ticket is €18.50. There are also boats here from Baiona. Timetables and tickets are on the websites www.mardeons.es and www.crucerosriasbaixas.com; it's worth buying them in advance at busy times. There's not a lot of shade on the islands, so take sunscreen; the breezy westerlies can be deceptive.

Listings Vigo and around *map p85*

Tourist information

In summer, an **open-top tourist bus** (www.vitrasa.es), does a circuit of the town, including stops at the two museums above and other attractions. A day's hop-on hop-off ticket is €7.50.

Vigo Tourist Office
At the heart of the waterfront area, Rúa Cánovas del Castillo 3, T986 224 757, www.turismodevigo.org. Daily 1000-1300, 1400-1700.
This modern office has plenty of helpful information.

Regional tourist office
Opposite the passenger terminal, Rúa Cánovas del Castillo 22, T986 430 577, oficina.turismo.vigo@xunta.es. Mon-Fri 0930-1400, 1630-1830, Sat 1000-1330.

Where to stay

There's plenty of accommodation for all budgets in Vigo, including a wide choice of chain business hotels.

€€€ AC Palacio Universal
C Cánovas del Castillo 28, T986 449 250, www.ac-hotels.com.

This noble waterfront building in the heart of town is a stylish modern hotel, with spacious rooms, and excellent facilities. Many of the rooms have great views over the port and the sea. You can pull up at the door, but get good instructions about how to use the automated car park opposite if you don't speak Spanish. There are often good offers for this hotel online.

€€€ Hotel Inffinit
C Marqués de Valladares 8, T986 442 224, www.inffinit.com.
With eye-catching modern design, this hotel has a fine central location and really comfortable, luxurious rooms with great bathrooms. The suites (€€€€) are really something to behold. Recommended.

€€ Compostela
Rúa García Olloqui 5, T986 225 528, www.hcompostela.com.
A quality mid-range hotel near the harbour, spruce and comfortable. It's got underground parking, important in Vigo, and there's friendly service and free Wi-Fi.

€€ Hotel Puerta de Gamboa
C Gamboa 12, T986 228 674, www.hotelpuertagamboa.com.

Right in the heart of old Vigo, handy for port, oyster street, and fish taverns, this small hotel is a beautiful conversion of a noble old building, with the combination of modern style and original features working well. Free Wi-Fi and cordial service, but no parking. Breakfast included. Recommended.

€€ Hotel Puerta del Sol
Puerta del Sol 14, T986 222 364, www.hotelpuertadelsol.es.
There's a bit of traffic noise, but this well-kept spot has plenty of character in its comfortable rooms, a good location at the top of the old town, and an underground car park right alongside. They've also got apartments at competitive prices, located opposite. It's significantly cheaper outside of high summer.

€ Hostal Buenos Aires
C Rosalía de Castro 6, T986 433 924, prbuenosaires@mundo-r.com.
A short stroll from the leisure harbour, this has large, spotless rooms with plenty of light and stylish modern bathrooms decked out with slate tiles. It's immaculate, and only the squeaky floorboards can be faulted. Great value year-round.

€ Hotel Aguila
C Victoria 6, T986 431 398, www.hotelaguila.com.
Central and friendly, this old hotel looks a little dilapidated at first glance, but the rooms – high-ceilinged and full of character – are spotless and have real charm. Prices are excellent for this location, and a simple breakfast is included, as is free Wi-Fi. A tip: turn off the air freshener before you go to sleep.

€ La Nueva Colegiata
Plaza de la Iglesia 3, T986 220 952.
A decent, cheap option in the old town with modernized facilities and bright, cheerful rooms that are a snip at this price. Expect street noise from the bars and restaurants nearby.

Restaurants

There are several good restaurants in Berbés around C de Carral, opposite the passenger terminal, and the nearby streets. Seafood terraces line C Pescadeira here. More upmarket choices are clustered in the streets behind the marina; C Taboada is a good place to start. C Olloqui, back from the Universal hotel, is another fertile tapas zone.

€€€ El Mosquito
Praza da Pedra 2, T986 224 411, www.elmosquitovigo.com.
This upmarket but down-to-earth and cheery restaurant in the old-town streets above the port has a deserved reputation for its seafood. Whatever you choose here is bound to be good; the octopus has an excellent reputation, as do the oysters and the *lenguado* (sole).

€€ Casa Esperanza
Rúa Luís Taboada 28, T986 228 615.
Warmly decorated and with a cordial welcome, this split-level place near the marina is a Vigo classic for the freshness of its seafood. Fish bursting with flavour and great shellfish make this a sound choice.

€€ La Trastienda del 4
C Pablo Morillo 4, T986 115 881, www.latrastiendadelcuatro.com.
A couple of streets behind the marina, this sophisticated wine bar and restaurant has a colourful summer terrace and an appealing interior

reminiscent of an old-time French grocers. The cuisine is innovative and imaginative, fusing styles and ingredients from around the world with success.

€€ Mesón El Capitán
C Triunfo 5, T986 220 940.
There's plenty of atmosphere and no nonsense at this excellent seafood eatery on one of the old town's major arteries. Whether you eat in the attractive upstairs *comedor* or downstairs by the kitchen, you'll enjoy top-notch *chipirones* on a bed of potato and onion, and a great *jarrete* (stewed lamb thigh), the house speciality.

€€ Restaurante Bitácora
Rúa Carral 26.
Good *raciones* of seafood in this smartish tapas bar and restaurant. You'll struggle to pass by without entering, the sizzling smells are so enticing. The *zamburiñas* in garlic are especially tasty. They also do a great seafood paella and decent *mariscada* for 2.

€€ Restaurante Don Quijote
C Laxe 4, T986 229 346.
This restaurant on a steep street above the passenger terminal is excellent, particularly its wooden outdoor tables. There's a full restaurant menu or excellent *raciones* and tapas; the *mejillones* (mussels) are particularly good, the *chipirones* are juicy and come with Padrón peppers, and the octopus is difficult to beat. Recommended.

€€ Vinoteca Cabernet
Teófilo Llorente 29, T986 227 429.
The best feature of this wonderful wine bar is its splendid vine-shaded flagstone terrace in the curious patio area, and it's a great discovery indeed in the middle

of old Vigo. Excellent wines, good cured meats and other tapas, and polite service. Recommended.

Cafés

Jackie's
Marqués de Valladares 14, T986 433 500.
One of Vigo's most popular breakfast spots, this busy café serves up strong coffee with a little wedge of madeira cake at its low bar, and also does tapas and has a cheap *menú del día.*

Bars and clubs

The bars of Berbés around Rúa Real get going at weekends. The classier joints around the marina see more mid-week action too, but are very pricey, particularly on the terrace. Most *discotecas* are near the train station.

Iguana Club
C Churruca 14, www.laiguana club.com.
One of the legendary live music venues of Northern Spain, with local and international rock bands on regularly. It's also a good spot for a drink, with 2 levels and a warehouse-like feel.

La Abadía de Santos
Off C Victoria.
A bar with an outdoor terrace located in a side alley that's the entrance to a church. Serves good beer.

Uno Está
Rúa Real 14. Tue-Sat 2200-late.
This solid stone building in old Vigo is occupied by this intriguing bar that is a light, airy space for a *copa* or professionally mixed cocktail, and frequently has live jazz or fusion bands, or DJs playing hip hop or electronica. Check their Facebook page for upcoming events.

What to do

Vigo's have-a-go football team, **Celta**
(T986 214 585, www.celtavigo.net),
are passionately supported. They don
their sky-blue tops at Balaídos, to the
southwest of town, normally on a Sun
evening. Tickets are available at the
stadium for a couple of days before;
the booth is also open a couple of
hours before the game.

Transport

Air
Vigo-Peinador Airport (VGO) is east
of the centre and connected with the
city by bus. There are flights from Vigo
to **Madrid**, **Barcelona** (including with
budget operator **Vueling**) and **Bilbao**,
while **Air France** fly direct to **Paris**.

Bus
The bus station is a good distance south
of the city centre, serviced by city buses
from Praza Puerta del Sol (No 9A). There
are frequent buses to **Pontevedra**,
leaving both from the bus station and
also from C Arenal 52 (25 mins). Buses to
Santiago leave every 30 mins, and there
are about 10 daily to **Ourense**. Buses

leave ½-hourly for **Baiona** and for **Tui**
and **A Guarda**. There are about 5 daily
buses to **Lugo** (4 hrs).

Among many long-distance
interurban services, there are 6 buses to
Madrid, 2 to **Bilbao**, 1 or 2 to **Barcelona**
and **Zaragoza**, 1 to **Salamanca**, **Gijón**,
and **Valladolid**. 4 buses Mon-Fri and
1 on Sat and Sun head to **Porto**.
Check www.autna.com for times.

Ferry
Vigo's days as a passenger port are just
about over, but there are still hourly
ferries to **Moaña** and ½-hourly to
Cangas, across the bay. In summer
boats go to the **Islas Cíes**, see page 86.

Train
Vigo's train station is at the eastern end
of town. Galician destinations include
A Coruña almost hourly (2 hrs), **Ourense**
7 times daily (2 hrs), and **Santiago** (1 hr
20 mins) via Pontevedra about 15 times
a day. There are good long-distance
connections. There is a Barcelona
sleeper, a day train to **San Sebastián** and
the French border, and a day and night
train to **Madrid**. There are 2 trains daily
to **Porto** (Portugal), and 4 a day to **León**.

South of Vigo

lovely Baiona boasts medieval walls and a spectacular fortress hotel

Baiona and around
Heading south, the elegant port and resort of Baiona is the main destination of
interest. On the way, **Playa América** is a long, narrow, popular and adequate beach
with a well-equipped campsite (see Where to stay, page 92).

Baiona is a beautiful spot, built behind a large, walled fort on the headland,
now a parador (an admission charge of €1 is haphazardly levied). It was mostly
built by the counts of Andrade, who bossed most of Galicia in their day, but
before that the headland was inhabited by Celts, Phoenicians and Romans. Take
the 3-km stroll around the impressive walls, reinforced with cannon, and have
a drink at the terraced bar; it's a superb spot, even if you're not staying in the
parador itself.

Baiona was agog in 1493, when the *Pinta*, of Columbus's small fleet, appeared at the port entrance with confirmation that the Atlantic could be, and just had been, crossed. There's a replica of the staggeringly small **Pinta** ⓘ *Wed-Mon 1000-1930, daily 1000-2100 in summer, €2*, in the port here, enlivened by a dummy crew.

On the hill above town is a giant and tasteless statue of the Virgin; you can, however, climb it for good views of the town and coast. Baiona has a small but colourful **tourist office** ⓘ *T986 687 067, turismo@baiona.org, winter 1000-1400, 1500-1900, summer 1000-1500, 1600-2100*, which is located by the entrance to the parador.

Oia

South of Baiona, the tiny village of Oia is a fairly untouched little fishing port. The licheny baroque monastery is in a poor way. The monks here knew about Oliver Cromwell's apocryphal advice to "put your trust in God but keep your powder dry"; they once repelled a Turkish pirate fleet with a volley of cannon fire. If you want to stay in this peaceful place, see Where to stay, below.

A Guarda

The last Spanish town on the Atlantic coast is A Guarda, a fairly uninspiring spot but worth visiting for the **Monte Santa Trega** ⓘ *€1*, high above town. Occupying the headland between the sea and the mouth of the Miño that marks the border with Portugal, it's a long but worthwhile climb (or drive). As well as great views over the town, river mouth and out to sea, you can pace the impossibly narrow streets of the ruins of a large Celtic town. One of the round stone dwellings has been reconstructed; the *palloza*, its direct descendant, was still a feature of many Galician villages until fairly recently. At the top, there's a chapel and a small museum with some finds from the site.

Listings South of Vigo

Where to stay

Baiona and around

€€€€ Parador de Baiona
Monterreal s/n, Baiona, T986 355 000, www.parador.es.
One of the chain's finest, superbly set in grassy gardens within the impressively walled fort on the headland. Comfortable rooms; many have great views out to sea. Recommended.

€€ Pazo de Mendoza
C Elduayen 1, Baiona, T986 385 014, www.pazodemendoza.com.

In the old dean's house in the centre of town, this is a characterful option and very good value for money. Rooms are equipped with modern conveniences but haven't lost the charm of this noble old edifice.

€€-€ Casa Puertas
Rúa Vicente López 7, Oia, T986 362 144, www.toprural.com.
A charming *casa rural* in a stone house in the narrow streets near the monastery. Rooms are simply furnished but comfortable, and offer great value in this peaceful village.

€ Hotel Caís
Rúa Alférez Barreiro 3, Baiona,
T986 355 643.
This friendliest of places is an unbeatable budget hangout. Right by the water, it has spacious rooms with TV and phone, and even a small swimming pool.

Camping

Camping Baiona Playa
Praia Ladeira, T986 350 035,
www.campingbayona.com.
A year-round campsite with cabins, a pool and all the trimmings on a long beach east of the town.

Playa América
Playa América, T986 365 404,
www.campingplayaamerica.com.
Mid-Mar to mid-Oct.
Campsite with bungalows and a swimming pool.

A Guarda

€€ Convento de San Benito
Praza San Benito s/n, T986 611 166,
www.hotelsanbenito.es.
This is an enchanting and peaceful place to stay, in a lovingly restored monastery with a pretty cloister. Have a look at a few rooms, as they are all quite different and have distinct charms; some are more expensive (€€€) and have hydromassage showers. Recommended.

Restaurants

Baiona and around
Pazo de Mendoza and **Casa Puertas** mentioned in Where to stay, above, are also reliably good eating places, as is the pricier parador.

€€ Jaqueyvi
Rúa Xogo da Bola 1, T986 356 157.
The corner bar is a great spot for ham and cheese tapas accompanied by local wine. Attached (or around the corner) is a sit-down restaurant with a good selection of Galician dishes, including excellent rices and *fideuàs* (similar, but made with noodles). There's also a fried fish eatery.

€€ Paco Durán
C Iglesia 60, Baiña, T986 355 017.
Up in the hills about 3 km from Baiona, this romantic spot has stupendous views over the bay and the Islas Cíes. There's great baked and grilled fish and very friendly service. Recommended.

Transport

Baiona and around
Bus
Buses run to/from **Vigo** every 30 mins. There are boats to the **Islas Cíes** in summer.

A Guarda
Bus
Buses leave for **Vigo** and **Tui** ½-hourly (fewer at weekends). There's a ferry across the Miño to **Portugal** and another crossing further east in Goián. The first bridge is at Tui.

Miño Valley

Rising northeast of Lugo, the Miño sweeps through much of Galicia in a southwesterly direction and forms part of the border between Spain and Portugal before it meets the Atlantic near A Guarda. Its lower sections run through a little-explored region of vineyards, monasteries and hidden valleys, watering the pleasant provincial capital of Ourense on the way.

Tui/Tuy
attractive border town with a lively nightlife and historic cathedral

Perched on a rocky hill high above the north bank of the Miño, Tui doesn't have the scurvy feel of most border settlements. It's an attractive, ancient Galician town that has exchanged growls through history with its counterpart fortress town Valença, across the water in Portugal. A former Celtic settlement, it was inhabited by Romans, then Sueves and Visigoths, briefly serving as capital of the boy-king Wittiza in the early eighth century. It was mentioned by Ptolemy, who named it Toudai and attributed its founding to Diomedes, son of Tydeus.

Sights
Tui has a solid assembly of attractive historical buildings, of which the highlight is the **cathedral**, which doubled as a fortress for so long. This function influenced the building's architecture, which has a military simplicity. It was started in the early 12th century and has both Romanesque and later Gothic features. There's a door of each type; the Romanesque portal has a simple geometric pattern, while the Gothic door and porch features an excellent sculptured Adoration, an early work with traces of colour remaining. It's flanked by later statues of the Elders of the Apocalypse. Inside are striking wooden beams; the church has a lean and has had to be reinforced over the years, especially after the 1755 Lisbon earthquake. The tomb of San Pedro González is here; he was a local Dominican who lived in the 13th century and cared for sick sailors, who dubbed him San Telmo after their patron. There's also an attractive cloister with a walkway above it that gives excellent views, as does the tower. There's a small **museum** ⓘ *1000-1330, 1600-2000, only weekends in Apr-May, closed Nov-Mar; cloister, tower and museum €3.*

There are several other churches in town and plenty of narrow lanes and fine old houses. It's a popular place with visiting Portuguese, and the town is well stocked with bars. There's a narrow, attractive road bridge from Spain to Portugal 1 km below the town; it was built by Gustave Eiffel in 1884. Although there's a depressing little border-bargain shopping area nearby, the town of **Valença** itself has several pretty corners, well worth ducking across to see.

Listings Tui

Where to stay

The luxurious Portuguese pousada just across the river in Valença makes another appealing base.

€€€ Parador de San Telmo
Av de Portugal s/n, T986 600 309,
www.parador.es.
Below the town, in a modern replica of a Galician *pazo* (mansion), the San Telmo offers good views of the town and river. It's a good place to relax, with a pool and tennis court among its conveniences.

Restaurants

€€ O Novo Cabalo Furado
Praza do Concello 3, T986 601 215,
www.cabalofurado.com.
One of the better restaurants, with cheerful and generous Galician *cocina de siempre*.

The lampreys from the river are delicious when in season; there are also decent (€€) recently renovated en suite rooms.

Transport

Bus
There are ½-hourly buses to **Vigo** and **A Guarda**, and some across the river to **Valença**. From A Guarda, the road follows the north bank of the Miño to Tui, and the first bridge into Portugal.

Train
The station, north of the centre, has 2 trains a day to **Vigo** and to **Porto**; it's easier to cross to **Valença**, where there are more trains into Portugal. Guillarei station, 30 mins to the east, has connections inland to **Ribadavia** and **Ourense**; a lovely trip.

Ourense/Orense

hot springs and pretty plazas dignify this underestimated inland city

Little-visited Ourense is the capital of Galicia's inland province (population 105,597), a rural zone crisscrossed by rocky hills and pastured valleys where much wheat is farmed and cheese and wine are made. The town itself is a prosperous centre with active streetlife. Once you get away from the busy roads and into the pedestrianized old town, it's a pleasant place indeed, with several beautiful plazas, and well worth a visit. A series of thermal springs make it a great spot to banish chills too.

Sights

The **Catedral de San Martiño** ① *daily 1130-1330, 1600-1930, Sun in afternoon only, free,* was started in the 12th century; most of its features are Transitional in style

Ourense

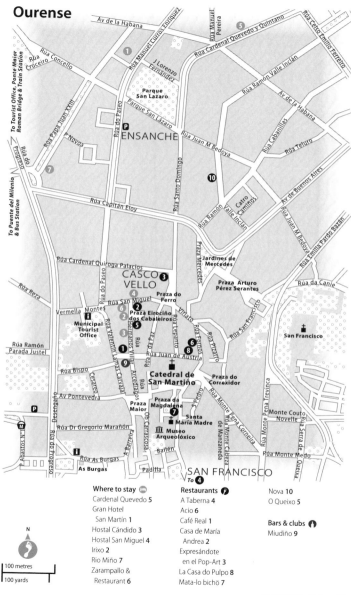

Where to stay 🛏
Cardenal Quevedo 5
Gran Hotel
  San Martín 1
Hostal Cándido 3
Hostal San Miguel 4
Irixo 2
Rio Miño 7
Zarampallo &
  Restaurant 6

Restaurants 🍴
A Taberna 4
Acio 6
Café Real 1
Casa de María
  Andrea 2
Expresándote
  en el Pop-Art 3
La Casa do Pulpo 8
Mata-lo bichó 7

Nova 10
O Queixo 5

Bars & clubs 🍸
Miudiño 9

BACKGROUND
Ourense/Orense

Although tradition claims that the city's name derives from *ouro*, meaning gold, it actually comes from the hot springs; the Roman town was named *Aquae Urentes* (warm waters). It was later an important city of the Suevish kingdom, and later of the Visigoths. As an important linking point between Galicia and the rest of Spain, Ourense flourished after its repopulation during the Reconquista. Following the decline that seemed to affect almost every city in Spain at some point, it is now a prosperous place, thriving as capital of this significant agricultural province.

(ie late Romanesque/early Gothic). The most impressive of the portals is intricately carved with scalloping and 12 good apostles below a headless Christ. The interior is long and gloomy, with many tombs of prelates carved into the walls; the attractive galleried cupola is a later early Renaissance work. There's an impressive version of Santiago's *Pórtico de la Gloria*, preserving much of its bright paintwork. The chief object of veneration is the *Santísimo Cristo*, a similar spooky Christ to the one in Burgos' cathedral. Made of fabric, the figure has real hair and a purple and gold skirt. It's located in a chapel that's an amazingly bright baroque fantasy in gold. Off the cloister is the **cathedral museum** ⓘ *Mon-Sat 1200-1300, 1630-1900, Sun 1630-1930, €2.*

The **Praza Maior** is just by here, a very appealing arcaded space. It's overlooked by the **Museo Arqueolóxico** ⓘ *T988 223 884, www.musarqourense.xunta.es, Tue-Sat 0930-1430, 1600-2100, Sun 0930-1430, free*, the provincial museum, very attractively set in the former bishops' palace. It contains many Roman and Celtic finds as well as some sculpture and paintings from churches in the province.

The pretty, linked **Praza da Magdalena** is off the main square and has beautiful overhanging buildings and roses. It's dominated by the cathedral and the **Iglesia de Santa María Madre**, an attractive baroque church built from the ruins of the 11th-century original; some Romanesque columns and capitals are preserved.

The main pedestrian streets to stroll down of an evening are the **Calle Santo Domingo** and the **Rúa do Paseo**. Fans of cream and brown should check out the latter; at No 30 the love-it-or-hate-it **Edificio Viacambre** looks like a Chinese puzzle box gone horribly wrong. The cloister of **Iglesia de San Francisco** is a beautifully harmonious Transitional piece of stonework, although each side has a different number of arches. The double columns are carved with capitals, many vegetal, but some featuring an array of strange beasts.

As Burgas and other hot springs

Below the old town, **As Burgas** ⓘ *Tue-Wed 0900-1200, 1800-2300, Thu 0900-1200, 1800-0100, Fri-Sat 0900-1200, 1900-0200, Sun 0900-1200, 1800-0100; free*, is the hot spring that attracted the Romans. The water streams out at a healthy 65°C. You can bathe open-air in the waters here, a great experience if the stares of passing tourists doesn't put you off. Take a towel and flip-flops. Nearby are some Roman ruins and the traditional food market, with plenty of outdoor stalls where farmers sell their produce. The Romans built a high bridge over the flood-prone Miño; it was rebuilt in medieval times and is still in use (Ponte Maior); it's worth the walk to see its elegant lines. Further along the river is the writhing metallic Puente del Milenio, a recent construction that's particularly impressive when floodlit.

There are several other hot springs along the river nearby, where you can bathe in the waters, particularly nice in the evenings for a relaxing soak under the stars. Some are upmarket spa complexes, others just pools in the ground. The temperatures vary, and some places charge a small admission charge. One of the best is **Chavasqueira** ⓘ *Mercado de la Feria s/n, T988 214 721, www. termaschavasqueira.com, Tue-Sun 0930-2330, to 0130 Fri night, to 0300 Sat night, €3.80*, which has free pools outside as well as a pay-to-enter complex. The nicest (and easiest) way to get to the springs is on the Tren das Termas, a 'train' that leaves the Praza Maior at 1000, 1200, 1600, 1800 and 2000 (hourly in summer) and stops at all the major springs, costing €0.75 each way. The tourist office has a good map/ brochure with the springs marked.

Listings Ourense *map p95*

Tourist information

There are a couple of useful tourist offices in Ourense.

Municipal tourist office
Rúa Isabel a Católica 1, T988 366 064, www.turismodeourense.com. Mon-Fri 0900-1400, 1600-2000, Sat-Sun 1100-1400.
Centrally located. There's also a friendly office with the same hours by the As Burgas hot springs at Rúa As Burgas 12.

Regional tourist office
At the southern (city) end of the Ponte Maior Roman bridge, T988 372 020, oficina.turismo.ourense@xunta.es. Winter Mon-Fri 0900-1400, 1630-1830, summer Mon-Fri 0900-1400, 1600-2000, Sat 1000-1400, 1600-2000, Sun 1000-1400, 1700-1900.
Quite a walk from the centre of town.

Where to stay

Ourense's hotels mostly offer exceptional value.

€€ Gran Hotel San Martín
Curros Enríquez 1, T988 371 811, www.gh-hoteles.com.
Looming over the park, this huge hotel may seem like some 1970s airport horror from the outside, but is much better within, although it still feels a bit old-fashioned and in need of a facelift. It has comfortable and well-equipped rooms, many of them with good views of the town. Excellent online deals can be found.

€€ Hotel Cardenal Quevedo
Rúa Cardenal Quevedo 38, T988 375 523, www.carrishoteles.com.
Stylish and spacious modern rooms, business-standard facilities and a decent central location make this welcoming hotel Ourense's best choice.

€€ Hotel Irixo
C Hermanos Villar 15, T988 254 620,
www.hotelirixo.es.
This hotel is ideal for those who want a base in the heart of tapas territory. It's decorated in a modern minimalist way, with lots of black and white. The rooms are correct and comfortable; those at the front get inevitable noise from the square, but it's great to be able to look out on the life below.

€ Hostal Cándido
Rúa Hermanos Villar 25, T988 229 607.
This has a good central location on a quiet square. The en suite rooms are large and have big windows and balconies; the furnishings are modest but comfortable enough. Good value.

€ Hotel Río Miño
Rúa Juan XXIII 4, T988 217 594.
This curious place offers remarkably good value. Despite the price, rooms are hotel standard, with small but modern bathrooms, telephones and TVs. The exterior rooms are a little lighter but have some noise. If there's nobody at reception, ask in the café.

€ Hotel Zarampallo
R San Miguel 9, T988 220 053,
www.zarampallo.com.
An attractive, central option above a good restaurant. The rooms are well equipped; there's a small price difference between those with a shower and those with a bathtub.

Restaurants

The Casco Vello is the centre for tapas-going and restaurants, particularly around Praza do Ferro, Rúa San Miguel, Rúa Viriato, Rúa Lepanto and Rúa Fornos.

€€€ A Taberna
Rúa Julio Prieto 32, T988 243 332,
www.ataberna.com.
With a modern presentation of classic regional Galician cuisine, this handsome place is Ourense's best restaurant at the moment. Both service and the wine list are excellent. Recommended.

€€€ Nova
C Valle Inclán 9, T988 217 933,
www.novarestaurante.com.
This contemporary, minimalist place is run by a group of young chefs. They offer 3 degustation menus, changing according to the season. Service, presentation and taste are all top-notch. Recommended.

€€ Acio
Rúa dos Fornos 1, T988 101 810.
You have to see the display of bartop snacks to believe it at this place. Gourmet creations cascade over each other in a devilishly tempting array, and there are good wines to accompany them.

€€ Casa de María Andrea
Praza Eirociño dos Cabaleiros 1,
T988 227 045.
An excellent option with a great location overlooking a pretty little square. The interior is modern and stylish; the upstairs dining area is arrayed around the central atrium and there's an excellent *menú del día* for €10.50, as well as filling *raciones* (€5-13) and a range of daily specials. Recommended.

€€ O Queixo
Pr Eironciño dos Cabaleiros 3,
T988 227 045.
Colourful original paintings and other objets d'art line this wood-beamed, stone-walled redoubt of comfort. A glass of wine comes with the bar's namesake tapa, a creamy soft local cheese. You can

also sit down and eat cheese, ham and sausage at tables.

€€ Zarampallo
R San Miguel 9, T988 220 053.
One of Ourense's better choices for a meal, with smart Galician fish and stews and a set *menú del día* for €10. Attractively modern interior.

€ La Casa do Pulpo
Rúa Don Juan de Austria 15, T988 221 005.
This friendly eatery is tucked away behind the cathedral. As the name suggests, its speciality is octopus, which can be eaten out the back. The bar has a selection of *pinchos* and little rolls; the calamari ones are particularly tasty. There's also a good selection of Galician wine.

€ Mata-lo bichö
Pl da Magdalena 7, T988 049 882, www.matalobicho.com.
With an excellent terrace, this sound modern tapas option specializes in grilled pig's ear or fried quail eggs with ratatouille and fried potatoes.

Cafés

Café Real
Rúa Coronel Ceano Vivas 3, T988 239 221.
An elegant, old-style café, very spruce and traditional with its polished wood and seriously impressive glass chandelier. 2 levels of seating and occasional live jazz.

Expresándote en el Pop-Art
C Santo Domingo 15, T988 255 756.
The name means 'expressing yourself through pop-art'. It's a flamboyant but relaxed café/bar popular with students, right in the centre of Ourense.

Bars and clubs

Most of the bar action is around Rúa Viriato, Rúa Pizarro, La Unión, Praza do Correxidor and the Jardines de Mercedes.

Miudiño
Rúa Arcediagos 13, T988 245 536.
This harmonious and low-lit stone and wood pub is just down the hill from the back of the cathedral. It's a very popular place for the first *copa* of the evening, and has Guinness on tap.

Entertainment

Teatro Principal, *Rúa da Paz 11.*
Has regular theatre and occasional arthouse cinema. Tickets are cheap.

Transport

Bus
Ourense's bus station, T988 216 027, is beyond the train station across the Miño from the old town; buses No 6 and No 12 make it out there. From Rúa Progreso, buses No 6 and No 12 go there. There are 6-7 daily services to all the Galician cities: **Lugo**, **A Coruña**, **Santiago**, **Pontevedra**, and about 10 services to **Vigo**.

Train
The train station is across the river to the north of town (20 mins' walk); from Parque San Lázaro dozens of city buses go in this direction.

Ribadavia

An excellent day trip from Ourense is to head down the Miño to Ribadavia, an attractive small riverside town that is the centre of the **Ribeiro wine region**. Ribeiro wines come both in a crisp white and a slightly effervescent red; both resemble northern Portuguese wines and are produced from the same grape varieties. The white *ribeiro* is the most common and is drunk all over Galicia out of distinctive white ceramic crucibles. The area was also notable for having been a profitable tin-mining zone.

Ribadavia is famous for having maintained a sizeable Jewish population from the 12th to the 16th century, even after the expulsion order of 1492. There are still some traces of the **Jewish quarter**; the old synagogue preserves many features despite its conversion into a church and the narrow streets remain, although nearly all the buildings postdate the era. A few Hebrew inscriptions and a Jewish pastry shop evince the town's pride in this part of their history.

The 12th-century **Iglesia de San Xuán** ① *Mon-Sat 0930-1430, 1600-1830, Sun 1030-1500*, has a Romanesque apse and curious portal of Mozarabic influence. The nearby Plaza Mayor is a fantastic long space, which harbours the helpful **tourist office** ① *T988 471 275, turismo@ribadavia.es, daily 0900-1330, 1600-2000*. The massive **Convento de Santo Domingo** ① *1000-1300, 1700-2000*, was once lived in by kings; the Gothic church and cloister is worth a look. The crumbly castle at the top of town is picturesque, but currently closed for running repairs.

The tourist office can furnish you with a guide to the region's *adegas* (bodegas) – one of the best ones to visit is pretty **Adega Casal de Armán** ① *T699 060 464, www.casaldearman.net*, which is open daily and has a restaurant and accommodation.

In early May, there's a wine festival in Ribadavia, and on the last Saturday in August, it's well worth attending the **Fiesta de la Historia**. The townsfolk are all dressed in medieval costume, and among other events there's a re-enacted battle and a real wedding in a medieval Jewish manner. Shortly afterwards, in early September, are the town fiestas.

North of Ourense

The **Monasterio de Santa María la Real de Oseira** ① *www.mosteirodeoseira.org, Mon-Sat 1000-1200, 1530-1730 (1830 summer), Sun 1230 and 1530-1730 (1830 summer), €2, guided tour only*, is often dubbed the 'Escorial de Galicia' for its immense size and harmonious Renaissance lines. Sitting solitary in a valley, it was founded in the 12th century and still houses a community of Cistercian monks in architectural splendour. The façade, from the early 18th century, is of monumental Churrigueresque style; the Virgin Mary occupies pride of place underneath a figure of Hope. Below is Saint Bernard, founder of the Cistercian order. The most interesting thing inside is the Claustro de los Medallones, carved with quirky depictions of historical figures. The austere church belies its baroque façade and is of little joy apart from some colourful 17th-century wallpaintings. Worth the journey on its own, however, is the Sala Capitular, with beautiful vaulting flamboyantly issuing from the twisted barbers-pole columns; it's like a fireworks display in stone.

East of Ourense

Off the main road east of Ourense is a beautiful gorge, the **Gargantas do Sil**, running up a tributary of the Miño. It's worth exploring by car or on foot; viney terraces soon give way to rocky slopes dropping steeply into the river.

The **Monasterio de Santo Estevo de Ribas de Sil** stands out like a beacon with its pale walls and brick-red roof against the wooded valley. Apart from the setting, the monastery isn't especially interesting, although there are three cloisters, one of them huge; another still preserves some Romanesque arching.

From near the monastery, the **GR56 long-distance trail** is a tough hike but a great way to explore some remote areas of Ourense province. It heads along the gorge and takes in another couple of monasteries along its 100-km route, before finally ascending steeply to the mountain village of **Manzaneda**, a small ski resort.

The N120 continues León-wards and bids farewell to the Miño just before the town of **Monforte de Lemos**. It's worth making a return train journey from Ourense to here, as the route is spectacular, running along the river and cutting into the Sil gorge for a short while. Monforte is dominated by a hilltop monastery (now a parador) and medieval tower that used to be part of a castle.

Near Monforte are the amusingly named wine towns **Sober** and **Canabal**. This is part of the Ribeira Sacra DO region, and produces both red and white wines, some of high quality. Beyond Monforte, there are several ruinous castles in the valley, including the **Castelo de Torrenovaes** looming over the road near **Quiroga**. There's a Roman tunnel near the road at Monferado. The last major settlement in Galicia is **O Barco**, a friendly but uninteresting town whose primary industry is the manufacture of *orujo*, a grape spirit which is popular across the region. It's consumed as a digestif neat or in its various flavour-infused versions, or added to coffee.

South of Ourense

South of Ourense, the towns of **Allariz** and **Celanova** are well worth a visit. Allariz flows down the side of a rocky *peña* that once housed a Celtic castro. The beautifully restored old town with its hilly flagstoned streets is picturesque and ideal for strolling. In the heart of it, the late 11th-century **Igrexa de Santiago** is a Romanesque church much modified in later centuries but conserving some interesting carved capitals around its apsidal windows. Other notable buildings included the **Convento de Santa Clara**, a muscular building by the central car parking space; it was founded in the 13th century but was extensively rebuilt after a fire in the 18th century. Across from it is the baroque church of **San Benito**. There's a little tourist office by the bridge at the entrance to town.

Celanova is known as the 'hidden city' for the reticence of its inhabitants, it's only a village really, dominated by the **Monasterio de San Salvador** ⓘ *Mon-Sat 1100, 1200, 1300, 1700, 1800 (also 1000, 1600, 1900 in summer), €1.20, guided tour only*, on a huge square. While the façade could be called over-ornate, the cloisters are a gem, dating from the 16th century. The Gothic wooden choir is also attractive. Around the back of the monastery is a Mozarabic chapel, **San Miguel**, a well-preserved 10th-century structure.

Some 25 km further south, the Visigothic church of **Santa Comba de Bande** is set above a long *embalse* (reservoir). It's a noble little structure with a small tower and square apse.

East of here, **Verín** makes a good place to explore and stay. It's an attractive walled winemaking town set in a valley, with an attractive church, and featuring a castle complex in the neighbouring village of **Monterrei** that was used in aggressions and defences against the Portuguese. There's a parador next to it.

Listings Around Ourense

Where to stay

Ribadavia

There are a couple of spa hotels within 5 mins' drive of Ribadavia but few choices in the centre itself.

€ Hostal Plaza
Praza Maior 15, T988 470 576,
www.hostalplazaribadavia.com.
By far the nicest place to stay in Ribadavia, this *hostal* is a clean, modern choice right on the beautiful main square, which some of the en suite rooms overlook. Recommended.

South of Ourense

€€€ Parador de Verín
Verín, T988 410 075, www.parador.es.
Opposite the castle in Monterrei, which more or less merges with Verín itself, this parador occupies a well-restored traditional rural Galician *pazo*. It's a good place for families, with plenty of space, gardens, a swimming pool and a lovely rose-edged patio. The rooms are excellent, and several boast super views over the fertile valley.

€€ Hotel O Portelo
Rúa Portelo 20, Allariz, T988 440 740,
www.hoteloportelorural.com.

On one of pretty Allariz's hilly streets, this excellent welcoming spot has very pretty rooms decorated in rustic style and taking advantage of the building's beautiful stone. There are modern facilities too, and a good breakfast available for a little extra. Recommended.

Restaurants

East of Ourense

€€ O Grelo
Rúa Campo de la Virgen s/n, Monforte de Lemos, T982 404 701, www.resgrelo.com.
An excellent spot with traditional food cooked with a sure touch. It's in a sturdy castellated building on the road leading up to the parador. Recommended.

South of Ourense

€€ Casa Fandiño
Rúa da Cárcel 7, Allariz, T988 442 216.
Just up from the church of Santiago in the heart of old Allariz, this is a great place to eat, a traditional restaurant serving up delicious Galician dishes like an *empanada de zamburiñas* (small scallop pie) or hake baked with peas, potatoes and onion. There's a *menú* for €15.

€€ Mesón O Candil
*Estrada 31, T988 411 120, www.
restauranteocandil.net, in the hamlet of
Pazos, on the road between the parador
in Monterrei and the town of Verín.*
An excellent choice for lunch or dinner.
It's simple in style, with a range of
parrilladas (mixed grills of meat or fish),
all of which are delicious, especially when
washed down with the house red, which
they make themselves. There's a pleasant
veranda to eat on in good weather.

€€ O Forno de Lito
*Pr de Cervantes 12, Celanova, T988 432
105, www.ofornodelito.es.*
This memorable spot specializes in
la pata de los poetas (the leg of the
poets), a deboned leg of beef, boiled
and crisped on a bed of *jamón* and fried
chorizo and lightly baked. Delicious, as
are the other roast meats on offer.

€€ Restaurante Brasil
*Av Castilla 7, Verín, T988 410 249,
www.restaurantebrasil verin.com.*
This traditional hotel-restaurant is an
excellent place to go for big portions
of quality fish and seafood at a more-
than-fair price.

€ Casa do Pulpo
Av Portugal 24, Verín, T988 410 886.
One of Galicia's best places to eat
octopus, this 75-year-old tavern doesn't
seem to have changed a bit since
it opened. No-frills wooden tables,
matronly Galician ladies cooking, cheap
local wine, and absolutely delicious
pulpo. Simple really! Recommended.

Festivals

Ribadavia
Last Sat in Aug Fiesta de la Historia,
see page 100.

Early Sep Town fiesta.

Transport

Around Ourense
Bus
Buses run very regularly to **Ribadavia**
(20 mins) and 2 daily to **Celanova**.
There are several buses to **Verín** and the
Portuguese border at **Feces**, and 1 daily
to **Porto**.
 Buses run eastwards to **León** via
Ponferrada, **Burgos**, **Madrid** 5-6 times
(6 hrs 20 mins), **Zamora** and **Salamanca**,
as well as other cities.

Train
A few trains daily head east to **León**
(5 daily, 4 hrs), **Madrid** (4 daily, 5-7 hrs),
and more distant destinations. 5 go to
Vigo (7 daily, 2 hrs) via Ribadavia and
A Coruña (4 daily, 2½ hrs) via Santiago.

Ribadavia
Bus and train
There are frequent buses and trains to
and from **Ourense** (20 mins).

East of Ourense
Bus and train
There are 6 daily trains on the
spectacular ride between Monforte de
Lemos and Ourense (40 mins). There are
also regular buses on this route.

South of Ourense
Bus
There are buses between Ourense and
Allariz more than hourly (30 mins). From
Verín, several buses a day head north to
Ourense and south to the Portuguese
border. Buses running between **Vigo**
and **Madrid** also pull in here.

Practicalities
Galicia

Best time to visit

The whole of Spain is busy in July and August and, while the north isn't ridiculously crowded, you'll need to reserve rooms in advance, for which you'll be paying slightly higher prices, and significantly higher on the coast. That said, it's an enjoyable time to be in the country as there are dozens of fiestas (Santiago de Compostela's main fiesta, the feast of Saint James, is on 25 July) and everything happens outdoors. It'll be pleasantly warm on the coast and in the mountains (although you're likely to see rain in both areas).

June is a good time too, with milder weather and far fewer crowds, as Spanish holidays haven't started. Spring (apart from Easter week) is also quiet, and not too hot, although expect coastal showers if not serious rain. Autumn is a good all-round time. Prices on the coast are slashed (although many hotels shut), and there are few tourists. The weather is unpredictable at this time: on the coast you could get a week of warm sun or a fortnight of unrelenting drizzle.

In winter, temperatures are mild on the coast and cold inland. Accommodation is cheap, but many places on the coast are closed.

Getting there

Air

With Spain going through tough economic times, many of Northern Spain's budget flight connections have been shut down, as local governments can't pay the heavy subsidies that some of these carriers demand. **Ryanair** flies to Santiago de Compostela from London, while **Vueling** links A Coruña with London. Both airlines also have a range of useful direct flights from right across Europe. If you're not on the budget carriers, however, it's often cheaper to fly to Madrid and connect via a domestic flight or by land transport. Madrid is a major world airport and prices tend to be competitive.

Domestic connections via Madrid or Barcelona are frequent. **Iberia** and its subsidiaries connect Barcelona and/or Madrid with most cities of the north, while **Vueling** and **Ryanair** also have useful domestic networks. If flying into Madrid from outside Spain, an onward domestic flight can often be added at little extra cost.

While budget carriers often offer excellent value (especially when booked well ahead), they offer very little flexibility. Be aware that if you're only booking a week or so in advance, it may be cheaper with other airlines. Cheap fares will usually carry a heavy financial penalty for changing dates or cancellation; check the small print carefully before buying a ticket. Some airlines don't like one-way tickets; it's (ridiculously) often cheaper to buy a return.

Before booking, it's worth doing a bit of online research. One of the best search engines for flight comparisons is www.kayak.com, which compares prices from travel agencies and websites. Another useful tool for its flexibility is at http://matrix.itasoftware.com, and www.opodo.com has up-to-date prices from a large confederation of airlines. To keep yourself up to date with the ever-changing routes of the bewildering number of budget airlines www.whichbudget.com is an option. www.ryalive.com is handy for searching for **Ryanair** connecting flights. **Flightchecker** (http://flightchecker.moneysavingexpert.com) is handy for checking multiple dates for budget airline deals.

Rail

Travelling from the UK to Galicia by train is unlikely to save either time or money; the only advantages lie in the pleasure of the journey itself, the chance to stop along the way, and the environmental impact of flying versus rail travel. Using **Eurostar** ① T0870 160 6600, www.eurostar.com, changing stations in Paris and boarding a TGV to Hendaye can have you in Spain 10 hours after leaving Waterloo if the connections are kind; calculate another several hours to reach remote Galicia. Once across the Channel, the trains are reasonably priced, but factor in £100-500 return on **Eurostar** and things don't look so rosy, unless you can take advantage of a special offer. Using the train/Channel ferry combination will more or less halve the cost and double the time.

If you are planning the train journey, **Rail Europe** ⓘ *T0844 484 064, www.raileurope.co.uk*, is a useful company. RENFE, Spain's rail network, has online timetables at www.renfe.es. Also see the extremely useful www.seat61.com.

Road

Bus
Eurolines ⓘ *www.eurolines.com*, runs several buses from major European cities to a variety of destinations in Northern Spain. From London there are several morning buses a week that pull into Bilbao some 21 hours later after a change in Paris. A return fare costs about £180; it's marginally cheaper for pensioners and students, but overall isn't great value unless you're not a fan of flying.

Car
The main route into Northern Spain is the E05/E70 tolled motorway that runs down the southwest coast of France, crossing into Spain at Irún, near San Sebastián.

Cars must be insured for third party and practically any driving licence is acceptable (but if you're from a country that a Guardia Civil would struggle to locate on a map, take an International Driving Licence). Unleaded petrol costs €1.50 per litre in Spain.

Sea

Bear in mind that from the UK it's usually cheaper to fly and hire a car in Northern Spain than bring the motor across on the ferry. For competitive fares by sea to France and Spain, check with **Ferrysavers** ⓘ *T0844 576 8835, www.ferrysavers.com* and www.ferrycheap.com, which list special offers from various operators. The website www.seat61.com is good for investigating train/ferry combinations.

UK–Spain ferries are run by **Brittany Ferries** ⓘ *T0871 244 0744, www.brittany-ferries.co.uk*, on three routes: Plymouth–Santander, Portsmouth–Santander, and Portsmouth–Bilbao. There's a twice-weekly sailing on each route, taking around 24 hours from Portsmouth and 20 hours from Plymouth. There's reduced service on the Plymouth route in winter. Prices are variable but can usually be found for about £70-90 each way in a reclining seat. A car adds about £150 each way, and cabins start from about £80. To use these services, you must be travelling with a vehicle.

Getting around

Public transport between the larger towns in Northern Spain is good; you can expect several buses a day between adjacent provincial capitals; these services are quick and efficient. The new network of high-speed **AVE** trains link major cities in double-quick time, but are significantly more expensive than the bus. Other train services are slow. If you want to explore much of rural Galicia, however, you'll probably want to hire a car or take a bike.

Rail

The Spanish national rail network **RENFE** ⓘ *T902 240 202 (English-speaking operators), www.renfe.es*, is, thanks to its growing network of high-speed trains, becoming a very useful option for getting around Northern Spain. AVE trains run between A Coruña and Ourense and there are other routes under construction. These trains cover these large distances impressively quickly and reliably. It is an expensive but excellent service that refunds part or all of the ticket price if it arrives late. Elsewhere though, you'll find the bus is often quicker and cheaper than the train.

Prices vary significantly according to the type of service you are using. The standard fast-ish intercity service is called *Talgo*, while other intercity services are labelled *Altaria*, *Intercity*, *Diurno* and *Estrella* (overnight). Slower local trains are called *regionales*.

It's always worth buying a ticket in advance for long-distance travel, as trains are often full. The best option is to buy them via the website, which sometimes offers advance-purchase discounts. You can also book by phone, but they only accept Spanish cards. In either case, you get a reservation code, then print off your ticket at the terminals at the station. If buying your ticket at the station, allow plenty of time for queuing. Ticket windows are labelled *venta anticipada* (in advance) and *venta inmediata* (six hours or less before the journey).

All Spanish trains are non-smoking. The faster trains will have first-class (*preferente*) and second-class sections as well as a *cafetería*. First class costs about 30% more than standard and can be a worthwhile deal on a crowded long journey. Buying a return ticket is 10-20% cheaper than two singles, but you qualify for this discount even if you buy the return leg later (but not on every service). A useful tip for the desperate: if the train is 'full' for your particular destination, try to buy a ticket halfway (or even one stop), get on, and then ask the ticket inspector whether it's possible to go further. You may have to shuffle seats a couple of times, but most are fairly helpful with this and you can pay the excess fare on board. Don't board a train without a ticket though.

An **ISIC student card** or **under-26 card** grants a discount of between 20% to 30% on train services. If you're using a European railpass, be aware that you'll still have to make a reservation on Spanish trains and pay the small reservation fee (which covers your insurance).

The other important Northern Spanish network is **FEVE** ⓘ *www.renfe.com* (now operated by RENFE but listed as a separate service), whose main line runs along the north coast from Bilbao as far as Ferrol in Galicia.

Bus

Buses are the staple of Spanish public transport. Services between major cities are fast, frequent, reliable and fairly cheap. When buying a ticket, always check how long the journey will take, as the odd bus will be an 'all stations to' job, calling in at villages that seem surprised to even see it. *Directo* is the term for a bus that doesn't stop; it won't usually cost any more either. Various premium services (called *Supra*, *Ejecutivo* or similar) add comfort, with onboard drinks service, lounge area in the bus station and more space, but cost around 60% more. Newer buses in all classes may offer Wi-Fi, personal entertainment system and plug sockets.

Most cities have a single terminal, the *estación de autobuses*, which is where all short- and long-haul services leave from. Buy your tickets at the relevant window; if there isn't one, buy it from the driver. Many companies don't allow baggage in the cabin of the bus, but security is pretty good. Most tickets will have a seat number (*asiento*) on them; ask when buying the ticket if you prefer a window (*ventana*) or aisle (*pasillo*) seat. There's a huge number of intercity bus companies, some of which allow phone and online booking; the most useful in Northern Spain is **ALSA** ① *T902 422 242, www.alsa.es*, which is based in Asturias and runs many routes. The website www.movelia.es is also useful. The platform that the bus leaves from is called a *dársena* or *andén*. If you're travelling at busy times (particularly a fiesta or national holiday) always book the bus ticket in advance.

Rural bus services are slower, less frequent and more difficult to coordinate. They typically run early in the morning and late in the evening; they're designed for villagers who visit the big city once a week or so to shop.

All bus services are reduced on Sundays and, to a lesser extent, on Saturdays; some services don't run at all at weekends. Local newspapers publish a comprehensive list of departures; expect few during siesta hours. While most large villages will have at least some bus service to their provincial capital, don't expect there to be buses running to tourist attractions such as monasteries or beaches; it's assumed that all tourists have cars.

Most Spanish cities have their sights closely packed into the centre, so you won't find local buses particularly necessary. There's a fairly comprehensive network in most towns, though; the Getting around and Transport sections in this guide indicate where they come in handy. In most cities, you just board and pay the driver.

Car

The roads in Northern Spain are good, excellent in many parts. While driving isn't as sedate as in parts of Northern Europe, it's generally of a very high standard, and you'll have few problems. To drive in Spain, you'll need a full driving licence from your home country. This applies to virtually all foreign nationals, but in practice, if you're from an 'unusual' country, consider an International Driving Licence or official translation of your licence into Spanish.

There are two types of motorway in Spain, *autovías* and *autopistas*; the quality of both is generally excellent, with a speed limit of 120 kph (130 kph in some sections). They are signposted in blue and may have tolls payable, in which case there'll be a red warning circle on the blue sign when you're entering the motorway. An 'A' prefix to the road number indicates a motorway; an 'AP' prefix indicates a toll motorway. Tolls are generally reasonable, but extortionate in the Basque country. You can pay by cash or card. Most motorways in Northern Spain, however, are free.

Rutas Nacionales form the backbone of Spain's road network. Centrally administered, they vary wildly in quality. Typically, they are choked with traffic backed up behind trucks, and there are few stretches of dual carriageway. Driving at siesta time is a good idea if you're going to be on a busy stretch. *Rutas Nacionales* are marked with a red 'N' number. The speed limit is 100 kph outside built-up areas, as it is for secondary roads, which are numbered with a provincial prefix (eg LU-552 in Lugo province), although some are demarcated 'B' and 'C' instead.

In urban areas, the speed limit is 50 kph. Many towns and villages have sensors that will turn traffic lights red if you're over the limit on approach. City driving can be confusing, with signposting generally poor and traffic heavy; it's worth taking a GPS or printing off the directions that your hotel may send you with a reservation. In some towns and cities, many of the hotels are officially signposted, making things easier. Larger cities may have their historic quarter blocked off by barriers: if your hotel lies within these, ring the buzzer and say the name of the hotel, and the barriers will open.

Police are increasingly enforcing speed limits in Spain, and foreign drivers are liable to a large on-the-spot fine. Drivers can also be punished for not carrying two red warning triangles to place on the road in case of breakdown, a bulb-replacement kit and a fluorescent green waistcoat to wear if you break down by the side of the road. Drink driving is being cracked down on more than was once the case; the limit is 0.5 g/l of blood, slightly lower than the equivalent in the UK, for example.

Parking is a problem in nearly every town and city. Red or yellow lines on the side of the street mean no parking. Blue lines indicate a metered zone, while white lines mean that some restriction is in place; a sign will give details. Parking meters can usually only be dosed up for a maximum of two hours, but they take a siesta at lunchtime too. Print the ticket off and display it in the car. Once the day's period has expired, you can charge it up for the next morning to avoid an early start. If you get a ticket, you can pay a minimal fine at the machine within the first half hour or hour instead of the full whack (though it must be said that parking fines are rarely pursued outside the city they are issued in, let alone in another country). Underground car parks are common and well signposted, but fairly pricey; €12-20 a day is normal. However, this is the safest option if you are going to leave any valuables in your car.

Liability insurance is required for every car driven in Spain and you must carry proof of it. If bringing your own car, check carefully with your insurers that you're covered, and get a certificate (green card). If your insurer doesn't cover you for breakdowns, consider joining the **RACE** ⓘ *T902 120 441, www.race.es,* Spain's automobile association, which provides good breakdown cover.

Hiring a car in Spain is easy but not especially cheap. The major multinationals have offices at all large towns and airports; the company with the broadest network is **National/ATESA** ⓘ *www.atesa.es*. Brokers, such as **www.webcarhire. com**, are usually cheaper than booking direct with the rental companies. Prices start at around €120 per week for a small car with unlimited mileage. You'll need a credit card and most agencies will either not accept under 25s or demand a surcharge. Rates from the airports tend to be cheaper than from towns. Before booking, use a price-comparison website like **www.kayak.com** to find the best deals. Drop-offs in other cities, which used to be ridiculously punitive, are now often much more affordable.

Cycling

Cycling presents a curious contrast; Spaniards are mad for the competitive sport, but comparatively uninterested in cycling as a means of transport. Thus there are plenty of cycling shops but very few bike lanes, though these are rapidly being constructed in most cities in the region. Contact the **Real Federación de Ciclismo en España** ⓘ *www.rfec.com*, for more links and assistance.

Motorcycling

Motorcycling is a good way to enjoy Spain and there are few difficulties to trouble the biker; bike shops and mechanics are relatively common. Hiring a motorbike, however, is difficult; there are few outlets in Northern Spain. The **Real Federación Motociclista Española** ⓘ *www.rfme.net*, can help with links and advice.

Taxis

Taxis are a good option; flagfall is €2-3 in most places (it increases slightly at night and on Sundays). A taxi is available if its green light is lit; hail one on the street or ask for the nearest rank (*parada de taxis*). In smaller towns or at quiet times, you'll have to ring for one. All towns have their own taxi company; phone numbers are given in the text.

Maps

The Michelin road maps are reliable for general navigation, although if you're getting off the beaten track you'll often find a local map handy. Tourist offices provide these, which vary in quality. The best topographical maps are published by the **Instituto Geográfico Nacional** (**IGN**). These are not necessarily more accurate than those obtainable in Britain or North America. A useful website for route planning is www.guiarepsol.com. Car hire companies have navigation systems available, though they cost a hefty supplement; you're better off bringing your own if you've got one.

    Stanfords ⓘ *12-14 Long Acre, Covent Garden, London WC2E 9LP, T020 7836 1321, www.stanfords.co.uk*, with well-travelled staff and 40,000 titles in stock, is the world's largest map and travel bookshop. It also has a branch at 29 Corn Street, Bristol.

Where to stay

There are a reasonable number of well-equipped but characterless places on the edges or in the newer parts of towns in Spain. Similarly, chains such as NH, AC, and Hesperia have stocked Northern Spain's cities with reasonably comfortable but frequently featureless four-star business hotels. This guide has expressly minimized these in the listings, preferring to concentrate on more atmospheric options, but they are easily accessible via their websites or hotel booking brokers. These things change, but at time of writing, by far the best booking website for accommodation in Spain was **www.booking.com**. If booking accommodation without this guide, always be sure to check the location if that's important to you – it's easy to find yourself a 15-minute cab ride from the town you want to be in. Having said this, the standard of accommodation in Northern Spain is very high; even the most modest of *pensiones* are usually very clean and respectable. Places to stay (*alojamientos*) are divided into three main categories; the distinctions between them follow an arcane series of regulations devised by the government.

All registered accommodations charge a 10% value-added tax (IVA); this is usually (but not always) included in the price and may be waived at cheaper places if you pay cash. If you have any problems, a last resort is to ask for the *libro de reclamaciones* (complaints book), an official document that, like stepping on cracks in the pavement, means uncertain but definitely horrible consequences for the hotel if anything is written in it. If you do write something in it, you have to go to the police within 24 hours and report the fact.

Hoteles, hostales and pensiones

Hoteles (marked H or HR) are graded from one to five stars and usually occupy their own building. *Hostales* (marked Hs or HsR) are cheaper guesthouse-style places that go from one to three stars. *Pensiones* (P) are the standard budget option, and are usually family-run flats in an apartment block. Although it's worth looking at a room before taking it, the majority are very acceptable. Spanish traditions of hospitality are alive and well; even the simplest of *pensiones* will generally provide a towel and soap, and check-out time is almost uniformly a very civilized midday.

Price codes

Where to stay

€€€€ **over €170**
€€€ €110-170
€€ €60-110
€ under €60

These price codes refer to a standard double/twin room, inclusive of the 10% IVA (value-added tax). The rates are for high season (usually Jun-Aug).

Restaurants

€€€ **over €30**
€€ €15-30
€ **under €15**

Price refers to the cost of a main course for one person, without a drink.

Most *pensiones* will give you keys to the exterior door; if they don't, be sure to mention the fact if you plan to stay out late to check that there'll be someone to open it for you.

Agroturismos and casas rurales

An excellent option if you've got transport are the networks of rural homes, called a variety of things, normally *agroturismos* or *casas rurales*. Although these are under a different classification system, the standard is often as high as any country hotel. The best of them are traditional farmhouses or old village cottages. Some are available only to rent out whole, while others operate more or less as hotels. Rates tend to be excellent compared to hotels, and many offer kitchen facilities and home-cooked meals. While many are listed in the text, there are huge numbers, especially in the coastal and mountain areas. Each regional government publishes its own listings booklet, which is available at any tourist office in the area; some of the regional tourism websites also list them. There are various websites listing some of them as well: search for "casas rurales" and you'll soon locate them. If you have a car, this can be a hugely relaxing form of holiday accommodation and a great way to meet Spaniards.

The Galician government publishes a listings booklet, which is available at any tourist office in the area; there's also a list on the tourism website www.turgalicia.es. The website www.toprural.com is another good place to find them.

Albergues and refugios

There are a few youth hostels (*albergues*) around, but the accessible price of *pensiones* rarely makes it worth the trouble except for solo travellers. Spanish youth hostels are frequently populated by noisy schoolkids and have curfews and check-out times unsuitable for the late hours the locals keep. The exception is in mountain regions, where there are excellent *refugios*; simple hostels for walkers and climbers along the lines of a Scottish bothy.

Campsites

Most campsites are set up as well-equipped holiday villages for families; many are open only in summer. While the facilities are good, they get extremely busy in peak season; the social scene is good, but sleep can be tough. They've often got playground facilities and a swimming pool; an increasing number now offer cabin or bungalow accommodation, normally a good-value option for groups or families. In other areas, camping, unless specifically prohibited, is a matter of common sense.

Food & drink

Nothing in Spain illustrates its differences from the rest of Europe more than its eating and drinking culture. Whether you're halfway through Sunday lunch at 1800, ordering a plate of octopus sometime after midnight, snacking on *pintxos* in the street with the entire population of Bilbao doing the same around you, or watching a businessman down a hefty brandy with his morning coffee, it hits you at some point that the whole of Spanish society more or less revolves around food and drink.

Eating hours are the first point of difference. Spaniards eat little for breakfast, usually just a coffee and maybe a croissant or pastry. The mid-morning coffee and piece of tortilla is a ritual, especially for office workers, and then there might be a quick bite and a drink in a bar before lunch, which is usually started between 1400 and 1530. This is the main meal of the day and the cheapest time to eat, as most restaurants offer a good-value set menu. Lunch (and dinner) is extended at weekends, particularly on Sundays, when the *sobremesa* (chatting over the remains of the meal) can go on for hours. Most folk head home for the meal during the working week and get back to work about 1700; some people have a nap (the famous siesta), some don't. It's common to have an evening drink or *tapa* in a bar after a stroll, or *paseo*, if this is extended into a food crawl it's called a *tapeo*. Dinner (*cena*) is normally eaten from about 2130 onwards, although sitting down to dinner at midnight at weekends isn't unusual. In smaller towns, however, and midweek you might not get fed after 2200. Be aware that any restaurant open for dinner before 2030 could well be a tourist trap. After eating, *la marcha* (the nightlife) hits drinking bars (*bares de copas*) and then nightclubs (*discotecas*; a *club* is a brothel). Many of these places only open at weekends and are usually busiest from 0100 onwards.

Food

While Galician cookery has its own differences and specialities, it remains an essentially Spanish cuisine. Spanish cooking relies on meat, fish/seafood, beans and potatoes given character by the chef's holy trinity: garlic, peppers and, of course, olive oil. The influence of the colonization of the Americas is evident, and the result is a hearty, filling style of meal ideally washed down with some of the nation's excellent red wines. The following is an overview of the most common dishes.

Even in areas far from the coast, the availability of good **fish and seafood** can be taken for granted. *Merluza* (hake) is the staple fish, but is pushed hard by *bacalao* (salt cod) on the north coast. A variety of farmed white fish are also increasingly popular. *Gambas* (prawns) are another common and excellent choice, backed up by a bewildering array of molluscs and crustaceans as well as numerous tasty fish. Calamari, squid and cuttlefish are common; if you can cope with the slightly slimy texture, *pulpo* (octopus) is

> Tip...
> See the Food glossary on page 128 for a guide to Galicia's cuisine.

particularly good, especially when simply boiled *a la gallega* (Galician style) and flavoured with paprika and olive oil. Supreme among the seafood are *rodaballo* (turbot) and *rape* (monkfish/anglerfish).

Wherever you go, you'll find cured ham (*jamón serrano*), which is always excellent, but particularly so if it's the pricey *ibérico*, taken from acorn-eating porkers in Salamanca, Extremadura and Huelva. Other cold **meats** to look out for are *cecina*, made from beef and, of course, *embutidos* (sausages), including the versatile *chorizo*. Pork is also popular as a cooked meat; its most common form is sliced loin (*lomo*). Beef is common throughout; cheaper cuts predominate, but the better steaks (*solomillo, entrecot, chuletón*) are usually superbly tender. Spaniards tend to eat them rare (*poco hecho*; ask for *al punto* for medium-rare or *bien hecho* for well done). The *chuletón* is worth a mention in its own right; a massive T-bone best taken from an ox (*de buey*) and sold by weight, which often approaches a kilogram. It's an imposing slab of meat, best shared between two or three unless you're especially peckish. *Pollo* (chicken) is common, but usually unremarkable (unless its free-range – *pollo de corral* – in which case it's superb); game birds such as *codorniz* (quail) and *perdiz* (partridge) as well as *pato* (duck) are also widely eaten. The innards of animals are popular; *callos* (tripe), *mollejas* (sweetbreads) and *morcilla* (black pudding in solid or liquid form) are all excellent, if acquired, tastes. Fans of the unusual will be keen to try *jabalí* (wild boar), *potro* (foal), *morros* (pig cheeks) and *oreja* (ear, usually from a pig or sheep).

Main dishes often come without any **accompaniments**, or chips at best. The consolation, however, is the *ensalada mixta*, whose simple name (mixed salad) often conceals a meal in itself. The ingredients vary, but it's typically a plentiful combination of lettuce, tomato, onion, olive oil, boiled eggs, asparagus, olives and tuna. The *tortilla* (a substantial potato omelette) is ever-present and often excellent. *Revueltos* (scrambled eggs), are usually tastily combined with prawns, asparagus or other goodies. Most **vegetable** dishes are based around that New World trio: the bean, the pepper and the potato. There are numerous varieties of bean in Northern Spain; they are normally served as some sort of hearty stew, often with bits of meat or seafood. *Fabada* is the Asturian classic of this variety, while *alubias con chorizo* are a standard across the region. A *cocido* is a typical mountain dish, a massive stew of chickpeas or beans with meat and vegetables; the liquid is drained off and eaten first (*sopa de cocido*). Peppers (*pimientos*), too, come in a number of forms. As well as being used to flavour dishes, they are often eaten in their own right; *pimientos rellenos* come stuffed with meat or seafood. Potatoes come as chips, *bravas* (with a garlic or spicy tomato sauce) or *a la riojana*, with chorizo and paprika. Other common vegetable dishes include *menestra* (delicious blend of cooked vegetables), which usually has some ham in it, and *ensaladilla rusa*, a tasty blend of potato, peas, peppers, carrots and mayonnaise. *Setas* (wild mushrooms) are a delight, particularly in autumn.

Desserts focus on the sweet and milky. *Flan* (a sort of crème caramel) is ubiquitous; great when *casero* (home-made), but often out of a plastic tub. *Natillas* are a similar but more liquid version, and *arroz con leche* is a cold, sweet, rice pudding typical of Northern Spain. **Cheeses** tend to be bland or salty. Though the standard Manchego-style cheese is still the staple of its kind (it comes *semi-curado*, semi-cured, or *curado*, much stronger and tastier), there are a number of interesting regional cheeses that are well worth trying.

Regional cuisine

Galicia is seafood heaven, with more varieties of finny and shelly things than you knew existed, usually prepared with confidence in the natural flavours. Inland Galicia relies more heavily on that traditional northern staple, pork.

On the seafood front, favourites are *percebes* (goose barnacles), *vieiras* (scallops), *zamburiñas* (queen scallops), *navajas* (razor clams) and various types of crab. Stew-type dishes are another local classic, and include *caldo gallego* (beans with cabbage, turnip leaves and pork) and similar *potes*. The *empanada*, a savoury pie of meat, fish or seafood baked between thick pastry in rectangular trays, is ubiquitous, and pork dishes like *lacón con grelos* (boiled ham with turnip leaves), or *churrasco* (ribs, also beef) are extremely popular. Small green Padrón peppers are normally deliciously flavoursome and mild, but the odd one famously has a hefty kick to it. Galician cheeses are well known across the nation, particularly the breast-shaped *tetilla*.

Eating out

One of the great pleasures of travelling in Northern Spain is eating out, but it's no fun sitting in an empty restaurant so adapt to the local hours as much as you can; it may feel strange leaving dinner until 2200, but you'll miss out on a lot of atmosphere if you don't.

The standard distinctions of bar, café and restaurant don't apply in Spain. Many places combine all three functions, and it's not always evident; the dining room (*comedor*) is often tucked away behind the bar or upstairs. *Restaurantes* are restaurants, and will usually have a dedicated dining area with set menus and à la carte options. Bars and cafés will often display food on the counter, or have a list of tapas; bars tend to be known for particular dishes they do well. Many bars, cafés and restaurants don't open on Sunday nights, and most are closed one other night a week, most commonly Monday or Tuesday.

Cafés will usually provide some kind of **breakfast** fare in the mornings; croissants and sweet pastries are the norm; freshly squeezed orange juice is also common. About 1100 they start putting out savoury fare; maybe a *tortilla*, some *ensaladilla rusa* or little ham rolls in preparation for pre-lunch snacking. It's a workers' tradition – from labourers to executives – to drop down to the local bar around 1130 for a *pincho de tortilla* (slice of potato omelette) to get them through until two.

Lunch is the biggest meal of the day for most people in Spain, and it's also the cheapest time to eat. Just about all restaurants offer a *menú del día*, which is usually a set three-course meal that includes wine or soft drink. In unglamorous workers' locals this is often as little as €8; paying anything more than €13 indicates the restaurant takes itself quite seriously. Most places open for lunch at about 1300, and stop serving at 1500 or 1530, although at weekends this can extend; it's not uncommon to see people still lunching at 1800 on a Sunday. The quality of à la carte is usually higher than the *menú*, and quantities are larger. Simpler restaurants won't offer this option except in the evenings. **Tapas** has changed in meaning over the years, and now basically refers to all bar food. This range includes free snacks given with drinks (now only standard in León and a few other places), *pinchos*, small saucer-sized plates of food (this is the true meaning of *tapa*) and more substantial dishes, usually ordered in *raciones* and designed to be shared. A *ración* in Northern Spain is no mean affair; it can often comfortably fill one person, so if you want to sample a range of things, you're better to ask for a half (*media*) or a *tapa* (smaller portion, when available).

Most restaurants open for dinner at 2030 or later. Although some places do offer a cheap set *menú*, you'll usually have to order à la carte. In quiet areas, places stop serving at 2200 on week nights, but in cities and at weekends people sit down at 2230 or later. A cheap option at all times is a *plato combinado*, most commonly offered in cafés. They're usually a greasy spoon-style mix of eggs, steak, bacon and chips or similar and are filling but rarely inspiring.

Vegetarians in Spain won't be spoiled for choice, but at least what there is tends to be good. There's a small but rapidly increasing number of dedicated vegetarian restaurants, but most other places won't have a vegetarian main course on offer, although the existence of *raciones* and salads makes this less of a burden than it might be. *Ensalada mixta* nearly always has tuna in it, but it's usually made fresh, so places will happily leave it out. *Ensaladilla rusa* is normally a good bet, but ask about the tuna too, just in case. Tortilla is simple but delicious and ubiquitous. Simple potato or pepper dishes are tasty options (although beware of peppers stuffed with meat), and many *revueltos* (scrambled eggs) are just mixed with asparagus. Annoyingly, most vegetable *menestras* are seeded with ham before cooking, and bean dishes usually contain at least some meat or animal fat. You'll have to specify *soy vegetariano/a* (I am a vegetarian), but ask what dishes contain, as ham, fish and chicken are often considered suitable vegetarian fare. Vegans will have a tougher time. What doesn't have meat nearly always contains cheese or egg.

Drink

In good Catholic fashion, **wine** is the lifeblood of Spain. It's the standard accompaniment to most meals, but also features very prominently in bars, where a glass of cheap *tinto* or *blanco* can cost as little as €0.80, although it's more normally €1.20-1.60. A bottle of house wine in a cheap restaurant is often no more than €5 or €6. *Tinto* is red (although if you just order *vino* it's assumed that's what you want); *blanco* is white, and rosé is either *clarete* or *rosado*. A well-regulated system of *denominaciones de origen* (DO), similar to the French *appelation controlée* has lifted the reputation of Spanish wines high above the party plonk status they once enjoyed. Much of Spain's wine is produced in the north, and recent years have seen regions such as the Ribera del Duero, Rueda, Navarra, Toro, Bierzo, and Rías Baixas achieve worldwide recognition. But the daddy, of course, is still Rioja.

The overall standard of Riojas has improved markedly since the granting of the higher DOC status in 1991, with some fairly stringent testing in place. Red predominates; these are mostly medium-bodied bottles from the Tempranillo grape (with three other permitted red grapes often used to add depth or character). Whites from Viura and Malvasia are also produced: the majority of these are young, fresh and dry, unlike the traditional powerful oaky Rioja whites now on the decline. Rosés are also produced. The quality of individual Riojas varies widely according to both producer and the amount of time the wines have been aged in oak barrels and in the bottle. The words *crianza*, *reserva* and *gran reserva* refer to the length of the ageing process, while the vintage date is also given. Rioja producers store their wines at the bodega until deemed ready for drinking, so it's common to see wines dating back a decade or more on shelves and wine lists.

Many people feel, however, that Spain's best reds come from further west, in the Ribera del Duero region east of Valladolid. The king's favourite tipple, Vega Sicilia, has long been Spain's most prestigious wine, but other producers from the area have also gained stellar reviews.

Visiting the area in the baking summer heat, it's hard to believe that nearby Rueda can produce quality whites, but it certainly does. Most come from the Verdejo grape and have an attractive, dry, lemony taste; Sauvignon Blanc has also been planted with some success.

Galicia itself produces some excellent whites too; the coastal Albariño vineyards produce a sought-after dry wine with a very distinctive bouquet. Ribeiro is another good Galician white, and the reds from there are also tasty, having some similarity to those produced in nearby northern Portugal. Ribeira Sacra is another inland Galician denomination producing whites and reds from a wide range of varietals.

One of the joys of Spain, though, is the rest of the wine. Order a *menú del día* at a cheap restaurant and you'll be unceremoniously served a cheap bottle of local red (sometimes without even asking for it). Wine snobbery can leave by the back door at this point: it may be cold, but you'll find it refreshing; it may be acidic, but once the olive-oil laden food arrives, you'll be glad of it. It's not there to be judged, it's a staple like bread and, like bread, it's sometimes excellent, it's sometimes bad, but mostly it fulfils its purpose perfectly. Wine is not a luxury item in Spain, so people add water to it if they feel like it, or lemonade (*gaseosa*), or *cola* (to make the party drink called *calimocho*). Tinto de verano is a summer slurper similar to sangría, a mixture of red wine, gaseosa, ice, and optional fruit.

Spanish **beer** is mostly lager, usually reasonably strong, fairly gassy, cold and good. A *caña* is a larger draught beer, usually about 200 ml. Order a *cerveza* and you'll get a bottled beer. Many people order their beer *con gas* (half beer and half fizzy sweet water) or *con limón* (half lemonade, also called a *clara*). In some pubs, particularly those specializing in different beers (*cervecerías*), you can order pints (*pintas*).

Spirits are cheap in Spain. Vermouth (*vermut*) is a popular pre-lunch *aperitif*, as is *patxarán*. Many bars make their own vermouth by adding various herbs and fruits and letting it sit in barrels; this can be excellent, particularly if it's from a *solera*. This is a system where liquid is drawn from the oldest of a series of barrels, which is then topped up with the next oldest, resulting in a very mellow characterful drink. After dinner or lunch it's time for a *copa*: people relax over a whisky or a brandy, or hit the mixed drinks (*cubatas*): *gin tonic* is obvious, as is *vodka con cola*. Spirits are free-poured and large; don't be surprised at a 100 ml measure. A mixed drink costs €4-7. The range of gins, in particularly, is extraordinary. There's always a good selection of rum (*ron*) and blended whisky available too. Spanish brandy is good, although its oaky vanilla flavours don't appeal to everyone. There are numerous varieties of rum and flavoured liqueurs. When ordering a spirit, you'll be expected to choose which brand you want; the local varieties (eg *Larios* gin, *DYC* whisky) are marginally cheaper than their imported brethren but lower in quality. *Chupitos* are shorts or shots; restaurants will often throw in a free one at the end of a meal, or give you a bottle of *orujo* (grape spirit) to pep up your black coffee.

Juice is normally bottled and expensive; *mosto* (grape juice; really pre-fermented wine) is a cheaper and popular soft drink in bars. There's the usual range of **fizzy drinks** (*gaseosas*) available. *Horchata* is a summer drink, a sort of milkshake made from tiger nuts. **Water** (*agua*) comes *con* (with) or *sin* (without) *gas*. The tap water is totally safe to drink, but it's not always the nicest; many Spaniards drink bottled water at home.

Coffee (*café*) is usually excellent and strong. *Solo* is black, mostly served espresso style. Order *americano* if you want a long black, *cortado* if you want a dash of milk, or *con leche* for about half milk. A *carajillo* is a coffee with brandy. **Tea** (*té*) is served without milk unless you ask; herbal teas (*infusiones*) are common, especially chamomile (*manzanilla*) and mint (*menta poleo*). **Chocolate** is a reasonably popular drink at breakfast time or in the afternoon (*merienda*), served with *churros*, fried doughsticks that seduce about a quarter of visitors and repel the rest.

Essentials A-Z

Accident and emergency

There are various emergency numbers, but the general one across the nation is now T112. This will get you the police, ambulance, or fire brigade. T091 gets just the police.

Electricity

Spain uses the standard European 220V plug, with 2 round pins.

Embassies and consulates

For a list of Spanish embassies and consulates, see http://embassy. goabroad.com.

Festivals and public holidays

Even the smallest village in Spain has a fiesta, and some have several. Although mostly nominally religious in nature, they usually include the works; a Mass and procession or two to be sure, but also live music, bullfights, competitions, a funfair, concerts, fireworks and copious drinking of *calimocho*, a mix of red wine and cola (not as bad as it sounds). A feature of many are the *gigantes y cabezudos*, huge-headed papier-mâché figures based on historical personages who parade the streets. Adding to the sense of fun are *peñas*, boisterous social clubs who patrol the streets making music, get rowdy at the bullfights and drink wine all night and day. Most fiestas are in summer, and if you're spending much time in Spain in that period you're bound to run into one; expect some trouble finding accommodation. Details of the major town fiestas can be found in the travel text. National holidays and long weekends (*puentes*) can be difficult times to travel; it's important to reserve tickets in advance. If the holiday falls mid-week, it's usual form to take an extra day off, forming a long weekend known as a *puente* (bridge).

Public holidays

The holidays listed here are national or across much of Galicia; local fiestas and holidays are detailed in the main text. These can be difficult times to travel; it's important to reserve travel in advance to avoid queues and lack of seats.

1 Jan Año Nuevo, New Year's Day.
6 Jan Reyes Magos/Epifanía, Epiphany; when Christmas presents are given.
Easter Jueves Santo, Viernes Santo, Día de Pascua (Maundy Thu, Good Fri, Easter Sun).
1 May Fiesta de Trabajo, Labour Day.
25 Jul Día del Apóstol Santiago, Feast of St James and the regional Day of Galicia.
15 Aug Asunción, Feast of the Assumption.
12 Oct Día de la Hispanidad, Spanish National Day (Columbus Day, Feast of the Virgin of the Pillar).
1 Nov Todos los Santos, All Saints' Day.
6 Dec Día de la Constitución Española, Constitution Day.
8 Dec Inmaculada Concepción, Feast of the Immaculate Conception.
25 Dec Navidad, Christmas Day.

Health

Health for travellers in Spain is rarely a problem. Medical facilities are good, and the worst most travellers experience is an upset stomach, usually merely a result of the different diet rather than any bug.

The water is safe to drink, but isn't always that pleasant, so many travellers (and locals) stick to bottled water. The sun in Spain can be harsh, so take adequate precautions to prevent heat exhaustion/sunburn. Many medications that require a prescription in other countries are available over the counter at pharmacies in Spain. Pharmacists are highly trained but don't necessarily speak English. In all medium-sized towns and cities, at least one pharmacy is open 24 hrs; this is organized on a rota system; details are posted in the window of all pharmacies and in local newspapers.

Hospitals

Clínica San Sebastián, Rúa Benito Corbal 24, Pontevedra, T986 867 890. Medical clinic with 24-hr attendance.
Hospital Juan Canalejo, A Coruña, T981 178 000.
Hospital Xeral, Rúa das Galeras, Santiago de Compostela, T981 950 000.

Language

→ See the language section on page 125 for basic Spanish words and phrases.

For travelling purposes, everyone in Northern Spain speaks Spanish, known either as *castellano* or *español*, and it's a huge help to know some. Most young people know some English, and standards are rapidly rising, but don't assume that people aged 40 or over know any at all. Spaniards are often shy to attempt to speak English. While many visitor attractions have some sort of information available in English (and to a lesser extent French and German), many don't, or have English tours only in times of high demand. Most tourist office staff will speak at least some English, and there's a good range of translated information available in most places.

While efforts to speak the language are appreciated, it's more or less expected, to the same degree as English is expected in Britain or the USA. Nobody will be rude if you don't speak any Spanish, but nobody will think to slow their rapidfire stream of the language for your benefit either, or pat you on the back for producing a few phrases in their tongue.

The other language you'll come across in Galicia is *galego* (gallego; Galician). Closely related to Portuguese, it's also pretty comprehensible if you know some Spanish.

Money

Check www.xe.com for exchange rates.

Currency

The euro (€) is divided into 100 *céntimos*. Euro notes are standard across the whole zone, and come in denominations of 5, 10, 20, 50, 100, and the rarely seen 200 and 500. Coins have one standard face and one national face; all coins are, however, acceptable in all countries. The coins are slightly difficult to tell apart when you're not used to them. The coppers are 1, 2 and 5 cent pieces, the golds are 10, 20 and 50, and the silver/gold combinations are €1 and €2.

ATMs and banks

The best way to get money is by plastic. ATMs are plentiful in Spain, and accept all the major international debit and credit cards. The Spanish bank won't charge for the transaction, though they will charge a mark-up on the exchange rate; but beware of your own bank hitting you for a hefty fee – check with them before leaving home. Even if they do, it's likely to be a better deal than exchanging cash. The website www. moneysavingexpert.com has a good rundown on the most economical ways of accessing cash while travelling.

Banks are usually open Mon-Fri 0830-1400 (and Sat in winter) and many change foreign money (sometimes only the central branch in a town will do it). Commission rates vary widely; it's usually best to change large amounts, as there's often a minimum commission of €6 or so. Nevertheless, banks nearly always give better rates than change offices (*casas de cambio*), which are fewer by the day. If you're stuck outside banking hours, some large department stores such as the *Corte Inglés* change money at knavish rates. Traveller's cheques are accepted in many shops, although they are far less common than they were.

Tax

Nearly all goods and services in Spain are subject to a value-added tax (IVA). This is only 10% for most things the traveller will encounter, including food and hotels, but is as high as 21% on some things. IVA is normally included in the stated prices. You're technically entitled to claim it back if you're a non-EU citizen, for purchases over €90. If you're buying something pricey, make sure you get a stamped receipt clearly showing the IVA component, as well as your name and passport number; you can claim the amount back at major airports on departure. Some shops will have a form to smooth the process.

Cost of living and travelling

Prices have soared since the euro was introduced; some basics rose by 50-80% in 3 years, and hotel and restaurant prices can even seem dear by Western European standards these days.

Spain can still be a reasonably cheap place to travel if you're prepared to forgo a few luxuries. If you're travelling as a pair, staying in cheap *pensiones*, eating a set meal at lunchtime, travelling short distances by bus or train daily, and snacking on tapas in the evenings, €65 per person per day is reasonable. If you camp and grab picnic lunches from shops, you could reduce this considerably. In a cheap hotel or good *hostal* and using a car, €130 each a day and you'll not be counting pennies; €250 per day and you'll be very comfy indeed unless you're staying in 4- or 5-star accommodation.

Accommodation is more expensive in summer than in winter, particularly on the coast. The news isn't great for the solo traveller; single rooms tend not to be particularly good value, and they are in short supply. Prices range from 60% to 80% of the double/twin price; some establishments even charge the full rate. If you're going to be staying in 3- to 5-star hotels, booking them ahead on internet discount sites can save a lot of money.

Public transport is generally cheap; intercity bus services are quick and low-priced and trains are reasonable, though the fast AVE trains cost substantially more.

Standard unleaded petrol is around €1.50 per litre and diesel around €1.40. In some places, particularly in tourist areas, you may be charged up to 20% more to sit outside a restaurant. It's also worth checking if the 10% IVA (sales tax) is included in menu prices, especially in the more expensive restaurants; it should say on the menu whether this is the case.

Opening hours

Business hours Mon-Fri 1000-1400, 1700-2000; Sat 1000-1400. **Banks** Mon-Fri 0830-1400; Sat (not in Aug) 0900-1300. **Government offices** Mornings only.

Safety

Northern Spain is generally a very safe place. Tourist crime is very low in this region, and you're more likely to have something returned (that you left on that train) than something stolen. That said, don't invite crime by leaving luggage or cash in cars. If parking in a city or, particularly, a popular hiking zone, try to make it clear there's nothing to nick inside by opening the glovebox, etc.

There are several types of police, helpful enough in normal circumstances. The paramilitary **Guardia Civil** dress in green and are responsible for the roads (including speed traps and the like), borders and law enforcement away from towns. They're not a bunch to get the wrong side of but are polite to tourists and have thankfully lost the bizarre winged hats they used to sport. The **Policía Nacional** are responsible for most urban crimefighting. These are the ones to go to if you need to report anything stolen, etc. **Policía Local/Municipal** are present in large towns and cities and are responsible for some urban crime, as well as traffic control and parking.

Time

Spain operates on western European time, ie GMT +1, and changes its clocks in line with the rest of the EU.

'Spanish time' isn't as elastic as it used to be, but if you're told something will happen *'enseguida'* ('straight away') it may take 10 mins, if you're told *'cinco minutos'* (5 mins), grab a seat and a book. Transport leaves promptly.

Tipping

Tipping in Spain is far from compulsory, but much practised. Around 10% is considered extremely generous in a restaurant; 3-5% is more usual. It's rare for a service charge to be added to a bill. Waiters do not normally expect tips but people will often leave small change, especially for table service. Taxi drivers don't expect a tip, but will be pleased to receive one. In rural areas, churches will often have a local keyholder who will open it up for you; if there's no admission charge, a tip or donation is appropriate (say €1 per head; more if they've given a detailed tour).

Tourist information

The tourist information infrastructure in Galicia is organized by the regional governments and is generally excellent, with a wide range of information, often in English, German and French as well as Spanish. Offices within the region can provide maps of the area and towns, and lists of registered accommodation, with 1 booklet for hotels, *hostales*, and *pensiones*; another for campsites, and another, especially worth picking up, listing farmstay and rural accommodation, which has taken off in a big way. Opening hours are longer in major cities; many rural offices are only open in summer. Average opening hours are Mon-Sat 1000-1400, 1600-1900, Sun 1000-1400. Offices are often closed on Sun or Mon. Staff often speak English and other European languages and are well trained. The offices (*oficinas de turismo*) are often signposted to some degree within the town or city. Staff may ask where you are from; this is not nosiness but for statistical purposes.

The regional tourist board of Galicia has a useful website, **www.turgalicia. es**, with extensive accommodation, restaurant, and sights listings.

Other useful websites

http://maps.google.es Street maps of most Spanish towns and cities.

www.alsa.es Northern Spain's major bus operator. Book online.

www.dgt.es The transport department website has up-to-date information in Spanish on road conditions throughout the country. Useful for snowy winters.

www.elpais.es Online edition of Spain's biggest-selling non-sports daily paper. English edition available.

www.feve.es Website of the coastal **FEVE** train service.

www.guiarepsol.com Excellent online route planner for Spanish roads, also available in English.

www.inm.es Site of the national metereological institute, with the day's weather and next-day forecasts.

www.movelia.es Online timetables and ticketing for several bus companies.

www.paginasamarillas.es Yellow Pages.

www.paginasblancas.es White Pages.

www.parador.es Parador information, including locations, prices and photos.

www.renfe.es Online timetables and tickets for RENFE train network.

www.spain.info The official website of the Spanish tourist board.

www.ticketmaster.es Spain's biggest ticketing agency for concerts, etc, with online purchase.

www.todoturismorural.com and **www.toprural.com** 2 excellent sites for *casas rurales*.

www.tourspain.es A useful website run by the Spanish tourist board.

www.typicallyspanish.com News and links on all things Spanish.

Visas

Entry requirements are subject to change, so always check with the Spanish tourist board or an embassy/consulate if you're not an EU citizen. EU citizens and those from countries within the Schengen agreement can enter Spain freely. UK/Irish citizens will need to carry a passport, while an identity card suffices for other EU/Schengen nationals. Citizens of Australia, the USA, Canada, New Zealand, several Latin American countries and Israel can enter without a visa for up to 90 days. Other citizens will require a visa, obtainable from Spanish consulates or embassies. These are usually issued very quickly and valid for all Schengen countries. The basic visa is valid for 90 days, and you'll need 2 passport photos, proof of funds covering your stay and possibly evidence of medical cover (ie insurance). For extensions of visas, apply to an *oficina de extranjeros* in a major city.

Weights and measures

Metric. Decimal places are indicated with commas.

Basic Spanish for travellers

Learning Spanish is a useful part of the preparation for a trip to Spain and no volumes of dictionaries, phrase books or word lists will provide the same enjoyment as being able to communicate directly with the people of the country you are visiting. It is a good idea to make an effort to grasp the basics before you go. As you travel you will pick up more of the language and the more you know, the more you will benefit from your stay.

Vowels

a	as in English cat
e	as in English best
i	as the ee in English feet
o	as in English shop
u	as the oo in English food
ai	as the i in English ride
ei	as ey in English they
oi	as oy in English toy

Consonants

Most consonants can be pronounced more or less as they are in English. The exceptions are:

g	before e or i is the same as j
h	is always silent (except in ch as in chair)
j	as the ch in Scottish loch
ll	as the y in yellow
ñ	as the ni in English onion
rr	trilled much more than in English
x	depending on its location, pronounced x, s, sh or j

Spanish words and phrases

Greetings, courtesies

hello	*hola*	please	*por favor*
good morning	*buenos días*	thank you (very much)	*(muchas) gracias*
good afternoon/ evening	*buenas tardes/ noches*	I speak a little Spanish	*hablo un poco de español*
goodbye	*adiós/hasta luego*	I don't speak Spanish	*no hablo español*
pleased to meet you	*encantado/a*	do you speak English?	*¿hablas inglés?*
how are you?	*¿cómo estás?*	I don't understand	*no entiendo*
I'm called ...	*me llamo ...*	please speak slowly	*habla despacio por favor*
what is your name?	*¿cómo te llamas?*	I am very sorry	*lo siento mucho/ discúlpame*
I'm fine, thanks	*muy bien, gracias*		
yes/no	*sí/no*		

what do you want?	¿qué quieres?	I don't want it	no lo quiero
I want/would like	quiero/quería	good/bad	bueno/malo

Basic questions and requests

have you got a room for two people?	¿tienes una habitación para dos personas?	when does the bus leave (arrive)?	¿a qué hora sale (llega) el autobús?
		when?	¿cuándo?
how do I get to_?	¿cómo llego a_?	where is_?	¿dónde está_?
how much does it cost?	¿cuánto cuesta? ¿cuánto es?	where can I buy?	¿dónde puedo comprar...?
is VAT included?	¿el IVA está incluido?	where is the nearest petrol station?	¿dónde está la gasolinera más cercana
why?	¿por qué?		

Basic words and phrases

bank	el banco	market	el mercado
bathroom/toilet	el baño	note/coin	el billete/ la moneda
to be	ser, estar		
bill	la factura/ la cuenta	police (policeman)	la policía (el policía)
cash	efectivo	post office	el correo
cheap	barato/a	public telephone	el teléfono público
credit card	la tarjeta de crédito	shop	la tienda
		supermarket	el supermercado
exchange rate	el tipo de cambio	there is/are	hay
		there isn't/aren't	no hay
expensive	caro/a	ticket office	la taquilla
to go	ir	traveller's cheques	los cheques de viaje
to have	tener, haber		

Getting around

aeroplane	el avión	left/right	izquierda/ derecha
airport	el aeropuerto		
arrival/departure	la llegada/salida	ticket	el billete
avenue	la avenida	empty/full	vacío/lleno
border	la frontera	highway, main road	la carretera
bus station	la estación de autobuses	insurance	el seguro
		insured person	el asegurado/ la asegurada
bus	el bus/ el autobús/ el camión		
		luggage	el equipaje
		motorway, freeway	el autopista/ autovía
corner	la esquina		
customs	la aduana		

north/south/ west/east	*el norte, el sur, el oeste, el este*	street	*la calle*
oil	*el aceite*	that way	*por allí*
to park	*aparcar*	this way	*por aquí*
passport	*el pasaporte*	tyre	*el neumático*
petrol/gasoline	*la gasolina*	unleaded	*sin plomo*
puncture	*el pinchazo*	waiting room	*la sala de espera*
		to walk	*caminar/andar*

Food glossary

It is impossible to be definitive about terms used; different regions often have variants.

For meats, *poco hecho* is rare, *al punto* is medium rare, *regular* is medium, *muy hecho* is well-done.

aceite oil; *aceite de oliva* is olive oil
aceitunas olives, also sometimes called *olivas*; the best kind are *manzanilla*, particularly when stuffed with anchovy, *rellenas con anchoas*
agua water
aguacate avocado
ahumado smoked; *tabla de ahumados* is a mixed plate of smoked fish
ajo garlic, *ajetes* are young garlic shoots
ajo arriero a simple sauce of garlic, paprika and parsley
albóndigas meatballs
alcachofa artichoke
alcaparras capers
alioli a sauce made from raw garlic blended with oil and egg yolk; also called *ajoaceite*
almejas name applied to various species of small clam
alubias beans
anchoa preserved anchovy
angulas baby eels, a delicacy that has become scarce and expensive; far more common are *gulas*, false *angulas* made from putting processed fish through a spaghetti machine; squid ink is used to apply authentic colouring
añejo aged (of cheeses, rums, etc)
anís aniseed, commonly used to flavour biscuits and liqueurs

arroz rice; *arroz con leche* is a sweet rice pudding
asado roast; an *asador* is a restaurant specializing in charcoal-roasted meat and fish
atún blue-fin tuna
azúcar sugar

bacalao salted cod, an emblematic Basque food; an acquired taste, it is worth trying *al pil-pil* (a light yellow sauce made from oil garlic, and the natural gelatin of the cod, very difficult to make, and Bilbao's trademark dish); *al ajo arriero* is mashed with garlic, parsley, and paprika
berberechos cockles
berenjena aubergine/eggplant
besugo red bream
bistek cheap steak
bizcocho sponge cake or biscuit
bocadillo/bocata a crusty filled roll
bogavante lobster
bonito Atlantic bonito, a small tuna fish
boquerones fresh anchovies, often served filleted in garlic and oil
botella bottle
brasa (a la) cooked on a griddle over coals, sometimes you do it yourself at the table
buey ox, or in Galicia, a large crab

cabracho scorpionfish
cabrales a delicious Asturian cheese similar to Roquefort
cabrito young goat, usually roasted (*asado*)

cacahuetes peanuts

cachelos boiled young potatoes, traditionally served with *pulpo* (octopus) in Galicia

café coffee; *solo* is black, served espresso-style; *cortado* adds a dash of milk, *con leche* more; *americano* is a long black

calamares squid

caldereta a stew of meat or fish; the broth may be served separate, like with a *cocido*

caldo a thickish soup

callos tripe

caña a draught beer

cangrejo crab; occasionally river crayfish

caramelos sweets

carne meat

carta menu

castañas chestnuts

cava sparkling wine, mostly produced in Catalunya

cazuela a stew, often of fish or seafood

cebolla onion

cecina cured beef like a leathery ham; a speciality of León province

cena dinner

centollo spider crab

cerdo pork

cerveza beer; *caña* is draught beer

champiñon mushroom

chipirones small squid, often served *en su tinta*, in its own ink, deliciously mixed with butter and garlic

chocolate a popular afternoon drink

chorizo a red sausage, versatile and not too hot

chuleta/chuletilla chop

chuletón massive T-bone steak, often sold by weight

churrasco barbecued meat, often ribs with a spicy sauce

churro a fried dough-stick usually eaten with hot chocolate (*chocolate con churros*)

cigalas The 4WD of the prawn world, with pincers; Dublin Bay prawns in English

cochinillo/lechón/tostón suckling pig

cocido a heavy stew, usually of meat and chickpeas/beans, typical of the mountains; *sopa de cocido* is the broth

codorniz quail

cogollo lettuce heart

comida lunch

conejo rabbit

congrio conger-eel

cordero lamb

costillas ribs

crema catalana a lemony *crème brûlée*

croquetas deep-fried crumbed balls of meat, béchamel, seafood, or vegetables

cuajada junket, a thin natural yoghurt eaten with honey

cuchara spoon

cuchillo knife

cuenta (la) the bill

desayuno breakfast

dorada a species of bream (gilthead)

dulce sweet

embutido any salami-type sausage

empanada a savoury pie, either pasty-like or in large flat tins and sold by the slice; *bonito* is a common filling, as is ham, mince or seafood

ensalada salad; *mixta* is usually a large serve of a bit of everything; excellent option

ensaladilla rusa Russian salad, potato, peas and carrots in mayonnaise

entrecot A juicy, fatty cut of steak, often from ox

erizos/ericios sea urchins; definitely an acquired taste, but strangely addictive
escabeche pickled in wine and vinegar
espárragos asparagus, white and usually canned
estofado braised, often in stew form

 F

fabada the most famous of Asturian dishes, a hearty stew of beans, chorizo, and *morcilla*
fideuá a bit like a *paella* but with noodles
filete a cheap cut of steak
flan the ubiquitous *crème caramel*, great when home-made (*casero*), awful out of a plastic cup
foie rich goose or duck liver from force-fattened birds.
frambuesas raspberries
fresas strawberries
frito/a fried
fruta fruit

 G

galletas biscuits
gambas prawns
garbanzo chickpea
granizado popular summer drink, like a frappé fruit milkshake
guisado stewed, or a stew
guisantes peas

 H

habas broad beans
harina flour
helado icecream
hígado liver
hojaldre puff pastry
horno (al) oven (baked)
huevo egg

 I

ibérico See *jamón*; the term can also refer to other pork products
idiazábal the Basque sheepmilk cheese, a speciality that sometimes comes smoked

 J

jabalí wild boar, usually found in autumn
jamón ham; *jamón de York* is cooked British-style ham, but much better is the cured *serrano*; *ibérico* refers to ham from a breed of pigs that graze wild in western Spain and are fed partly on acorns (*bellotas*) Particular regions and villages are known for their hams, which can get mighty expensive
judías verdes green beans

 K

kokotxas pieces of hake cheek and throat, cooked in a rich sauce; usually delicious, if a little fatty

 L

lacón con grelos Galician stew of pork and potatoes
langosta crayfish
langostinos king prawns
lechazo milk-fed lamb
leche milk
lechuga lettuce
lenguado sole
lentejas lentils
limón lemon
lomo loin, usually sliced pork
longaniza long sausage; an Aragón speciality
lubina sea bass

M

macedonia de frutas fruit salad, usually tinned

magret de pato fattened duck breast

manchego Spain's national cheese; hard, whitish, and made from ewe's milk

mantequilla butter

manzana apple

manzanilla a word referring to the nicest type of olive; also camomile; and a dry wine similar to sherry

marisco shellfish

matanza (la) early Nov is pig-killing time, with much feasting and many pork products

mejillones mussels

melocotón peach, usually canned and served in *almibar* (syrup)

membrillo quince jelly, usually eaten with cheese

menestra a vegetable stew, usually served like a minestrone without the liquid; vegetarians will be annoyed to find that it's often seeded with ham and bits of pork

menú a set meal, usually consisting of three or more courses, bread and wine or water

merluza hake is to Spain as rice is to southeast Asia

miel honey

mollejas sweetbreads; ie the pancreas or neck glands of a calf or lamb

migas breadcrumbs, fried and often mixed with lard and meat to form a delicious peasant dish of the same name

morcilla blood sausage, either solid or semi-liquid; a speciality of León and Burgos

morro cheek, pork or lamb

mostaza mustard

mosto grape juice, a common option in bars

N

naranja orange

nata sweet whipped cream

navajas razor-shells

natillas rich custard dessert

nécora small sea crab, sometimes called a velvet crab

nueces walnuts

O

orejas ears, usually of a pig

orujo a fiery grape spirit, often brought to add to coffee if the waiter likes you

ostra oyster

P

pan bread

parrilla grill; a *parrillada* is a mixed grill

pastel cake/pastry

patatas potatoes; often chips (*patatas fritas*); *bravas* are with spicy sauce; *a la Riojana* is with paprika and chorizo

pato duck

patxarán the sloe-berry, but usually the liqueur made from it, often flavoured with *anis*; some are fairly medicinal, most light, fruity and delicious

pechuga breast (usually chicken)

perdiz partridge

percebes goose-neck barnacles, a curious speciality of Galicia; salty and tasty, but tough to open

pescado fish

picadillo a dish of spicy mincemeat

picante spicy hot

pichón squab

pimienta pepper

pimientos peppers; there are many kinds; *piquillos* are the trademark thin Basque red pepper; Padrón produces sweet green mini ones; Bierzo loves theirs stuffed *rellenos*

pintxo/pincho the reason you put on weight in the Basque country; bartop snack

pipas sunflower seeds, a common snack

plancha (a la) grilled on a hot iron

plátano banana

pochas young haricot beans, a Riojan speciality

pollo chicken

postre dessert

puerros leeks

pulga a colloquial word for the tiny submarine-shaped rolls that feature atop bars in the Basque lands; the word actually means 'flea'

pulpo octopus, particularly delicious *a la gallega*, boiled Galician style and garnished with olive oil, salt, and paprika

queimada a potent Galician ritual drink of *orujo* mixed with coffee and then heated over a fire

queso cheese

rabas crumbed calamari strips, often eaten at weekends

rabo de buey oxtail

ración a portion of food served in cafés and bars; check the size and order a half (*media*) if you want less

rana frog; *ancas de rana* is frogs' legs

rape monkfish/anglerfish

relleno/a stuffed

reserva, gran reserva, crianza, cosechero terms relating to the age of wines; see page 117

revuelto scrambled eggs, usually with mushrooms or seafood; often a speciality

riñones kidneys

rodaballo turbot; pricey and delicious

romana (*a la*) fried in batter

sagardotegi cider house in the Basque country

sal salt

salchichón a salami-like sausage

salmón salmon

salpicón a seafood salad with plenty of onion and vinegar

San Jacobo a steak cooked with ham and cheese

sardiñas sardines, delicious grilled

seco dry

sepia cuttlefish

serrano see *jamón*

setas wild mushrooms, often superb

sidra cider

solomillo beef fillet steak cut from the sirloin bone

sopa soup

tarta tart or cake

té tea

tenedor fork

ternera veal or young beef

tocino pork fat; *tocinillo del cielo* is an excellent caramelized egg dessert

tomate tomato

tortilla a Spanish omelette, with potato, egg, olive oil and optional onion

trucha trout; *a la Navarra* comes with bacon or ham

toro a traditional Basque fish stew or soup

txaka/chaka a mixture of mayonnaise and chopped seafood, featuring heavily in *pintxos*

txakolí slightly effervescent Basque wine produced from underripe grapes

txangurro spider crab, superb

uva grape

V

vaso glass
verduras vegetables
vermut vermouth; delicious when it's the bar's own. Traditionally drunk at weekends before lunch – *la hora de vermut*.
vieiras scallops, also called *veneras*
vino wine; *blanco* is white, *rosado* or *clarete* is rosé, *tinto* is red
vizcaína (a la) in the style of Vizcaya, Bilbao's province; usually based on onions and dried peppers

X

xoubas sardines in Galicia

Z

zamburiñas a type of small scallop
zanahoria carrot
zumo fruit juice, usually bottled and pricey
zurito a short beer in the Basque country, useful for tapas-hopping; varies in size from a splash to a quarter-pint

Index → *Entries in* **bold** *refer to maps*

FOOTPRINT

Features

Credits

Footprint credits
Editor: Nicola Gibbs
Production and layout: Emma Bryers
Maps: Kevin Feeney
Colour section: Angus Dawson

Publisher: Patrick Dawson
Managing Editor: Felicity Laughton
Administration: Elizabeth Taylor
Advertising sales and marketing:
John Sadler, Kirsty Holmes,
Debbie Wylde

Photography credits
Front cover: Luis Cagiao/
Shutterstock.com
Back cover: Top: Migel/Shutterstock.com.
Bottom: Guillermo del Olmo/
Shutterstock.com

Colour section
Inside front cover: age fotostock/
Superstock, Robert Harding Picture
Library/Superstock
Page 1: Hemis.fr/Superstock
Page 2: Anibal Trejo/Shutterstock.com
Page 4: Botond Horvath/
Shutterstock.com
Page 5: FCG/Shutterstock.com,
Anibal Trejo/Superstock,
Juan Carlos Cantero/Superstock

Printed in Spain by GraphyCems

Publishing information
Footprint Galicia
2nd edition
© Footprint Handbooks Ltd
July 2015

ISBN: 978 1 910120 48 4
CIP DATA: A catalogue record for this
book is available from the British Library

® Footprint Handbooks and the
Footprint mark are a registered
trademark of Footprint Handbooks Ltd

Published by Footprint
6 Riverside Court
Lower Bristol Road
Bath BA2 3DZ, UK
T +44 (0)1225 469141
F +44 (0)1225 469461
footprinttravelguides.com

Distributed in the USA by
National Book Network, Inc.